Vermont Valley

VERMONT VALLEY

by Walter Hard

HARCOURT, BRACE AND COMPANY

NEW YORK

Typography by Robert Josephy

PRINTED IN THE UNITED STATES OF AMERICA
BY QUINN & BODEN COMPANY, INC., RAHWAY, N. J.

For Margaret Hard

"I should be willing to say . . .
That once you had opened the valley's singing day."

ROBERT FROST

Acknowledgment is made to the *Rutland Herald* and the *Manchester Journal* in which many of these poems have appeared.

Contents

Vermont Valley

The Mountain Farm

The farm lay along the slope of the mountain
Which rose gently from the upper meadows.
What Sam Parker got from it
He wrested by main force:
Not that the land was poor,
But it was in such small pieces
With limestone ledges cropping out between.
It was one of those farms
Which never should have been divorced from the forest
Which still hovered on its flanks.
And yet three generations had lived there
And Sam's children showed no signs of want.

One summer day a man drove by
And stopped, as many did, to get the view.
The valley, a green bowl miles wide.
North, south, and east, the uneven rim of mountains,
Everchanging, eternal.
The V-shaped nick to the south
Was where Stark marched his men
On the way to the Battle of Bennington.

The next day the man came again
And brought Howard Stickles,
A lawyer who made his living
By selling insurance and real estate—
Mostly timberland until the city folks
Began to buy up abandoned farms.
After some general talk

3

He asked Sam if he'd ever thought of selling:
His client, here, sort of took a fancy to the view.
The upshot of it was the man made an offer
Of fifteen thousand dollars for the farm.
Stunned by just the name of so much money,
Sam asked for time to talk it over with his wife.
That night when the children were asleep upstairs,
Sam and his wife talked and planned.
They remembered all the things they'd gone without,
The hard days and wakeful nights.
These they weighed against the joys,
The real rewards of honest toil,
And the memories haunting every corner of the old
   house.
But then the freedom fifteen thousand dollars meant:
A better farm near town, and money in the bank.
Almost decided to sell, Sam lit his lantern
And went out for his nightly inspection of the barns.
Coming back he stopped on the porch.
A full moon was brooding over the sleeping valley.
He could see the mountain peaks
Gray and calm in the silvery summer night.

Here and there a light twinkled—
His neighbors though miles apart.
He called his wife.
They stood together
Awestruck at the mystery which is night among the
   mountains.
A horse pounded in his stall.
A calf bleated and its mother answered.

4

A dog barked,
And then the silence of the moonlit valley

The next morning coming from the creamery,
Sam saw Stickles and the man.
"The woman and I've decided.
We don't want to let the old place go.
What'd I do with fifteen thousand dollars anyhow?
It'd just be a worriment."

Golden Silence

It wasn't more than an hour
After three people had been seen
Coming out of Lawyer Bullard's office
That everybody in the village
Knew there was some scandal over in The Hollow.
The storekeeper's wife told him what she thought of him
For not bringing any news when he came to supper.
He admitted that Polk Huggins had been in,
But he'd never thought to ask him the news,
Although he'd seen Polk and the others from The Hol-
　　low
Coming out of the law office, too.
His wife didn't even stop to do up the supper dishes,
But rushed right across the street to tell Stella Hun
Just how stupid men were.

The next morning Stella Hun started on foot
To go to The Hollow to learn the truth.
She got a ride with a boy coming from the creamery,
So she landed in front of Polk Huggins' house
Before Mrs. Huggins had done with her kitchen work.

It was well toward noon when Stella shut the gate
In the Huggins' fence.
All she had been able to get out of Mrs. Huggins
Was that Polk had said, when she asked him,
That he guessed there "wa'n't much to it wuth talkin' of."
"You know," Mrs. Huggins had added, "Polk ain't one
　　to talk."

Stella, back in the village, was sipping tea
While she tried to make some sort of news
For the storekeeper's wife,
Who hovered around in expectation.
Finally Stella put her cup down and looked out of the
    window.
"My lands! I don't know whether Polk Higgins
Is so tight-mouthed jest 'cause he won't tell nothin',
Er whether he jest ain't got nothin' in his head
To let out his mouth."

The storekeeper's wife told him about Stella's call
That night. He looked up from his paper:
"She don't know whether he's a damned fool
Er jest a fool, does she?"

They Also Serve

"Well, well! So he gave that Town Hall
In memory of his father and mother?
You don't say! Born on that back-hill farm?
Started from that—and now look at this!
You say his brother still lives up there?
I see. Probably never amounted to much."
Or someone else will reply:
"Sister? Oh, yes.
She had considerable schooling, too,
But she came back and lived on the farm;
Taught some in Number 9 District."

How often when there is talk of Vermont's great sons,
Who have done things in the world,
Someone who stayed at home comes in.
For instance, there was Ellen Twitchell.
Of course, since Henry made his money
She's well taken care of—
But before his ship came in
It was Ellen who kept things going at home.
She'd been at college about two years
When her father had that stroke,
And she came back and took charge of things.
After he died she did a man's work.

I don't mean to belittle greatness,
But just to call to mind
That greatness isn't a one-man job.
So when you're calling the roll
Don't forget the Ellen Twitchells.

8

Then sometimes you'll hear this:
"You don't mean to tell me!
So that fellow is a brother?
Well, it's evident the Judge had all the brains
Of that family."

Perhaps he did.
Ed Slicer made a fine record as a lawyer
Before he became famous as a judge.
He deserves all the praise his proud state offers.
John, the brother, wasn't much of a scholar;
What little he got came hard.
His bent was mechanics,
But when he wanted to go and get a training,
Ed was still in college.
Someone had to carry on the farm—
The old folks couldn't do it alone—
So John stayed at home.
Of course, it was right. John knew that.

All I am saying is:
When you're calling the roll
Of men who have gone out from these farms
And done the nation service,
Don't forget the others—
Those who had the brains
To know brains when they saw them;
Those who were big enough
Not to amount to much.

A Good Waiter

Aldous didn't belong to the Grange.
He always said he "callated" to someday,
But up to sixty-four he hadn't gotten around to it.
He'd been on every Grange picnic for years though,
And in winter he went to their suppers
And never failed to eat his share of the food.
When you stopped to think of it
You realized that Aldous was usually around,
Ready to partake of any pleasure
As long as somebody else furnished it.
Even at barn-raisings, in the old times,
They said Aldous was handy at giving orders
And was always rushing hither and yon.
The only time he was known to accomplish anything
Was when the food was passed around—
And, of course, he did hold his own on the cider.

Last year he somehow got a ride over to the lake
And by the time the Grangers began to arrive
Aldous already was a part of the picnic.
He was gathering sticks for the fire;
He'd pick up two or three he could break easily
And carefully pile them near the stone fireplace.
As soon as the crowd appeared he retired to a soft spot
Under a pine where he rested peacefully.
When the men began to line up with their paper plates
Somebody called to Aldous, resting under his tree,
"Aldous, you'd better get up and into line."
Aldous leaned on his elbow.

"Young feller," he said, "I've lived long enough
Under this administration
T' know if I set here long enough
It'll be fetched t' me."

Lampson's Descent

The slope below Table Rock
Is hard enough to climb in summer.
In winter when the ground is hard,
Or the crust is strong enough to hold,
Climbing up it is a hand-and-knee journey.
We'd been cutting near the top
Where a stand of hard wood grew.
I had been working an hour or so one morning
When I heard Lampson coming up the grade
Whistling as usual.
I could tell when he began to climb
By the lack of steam behind his whistle.
He got near the top
When all at once his whistle stopped.
I heard a sound like ripping cloth—
And then nothing but the drip of water
From the ledge above.
I dropped my ax.
He might be hurt.
I stood and listened on the ridge.
Then I heard him pulling up again,
Crunching the snow with a determined heel.
Slowly he drew near.
Not wanting him to know I knew
About his swift descent,
I went back to my chopping
And looked surprised when he appeared,
Puffing and blowing.
He dumped himself on an old black stump

And lit his clay, covering the bowl with his fingers
To make it draw better. "Wallace," he said,
"I don't think much o' these ideas
The Labor Unions 're allays preachin'
'Bout hours o' labor.
They talk too much 'bout time
And not a word o' finishin' the job.
I s'pose it's based on Scriptur though."
He puffed and spat. And then:
"I don't mean t' be erreverent y' know
By referrin' t' Scriptur, but I was thinkin',
As I come up the hill—the second trip.
They say the Creator made th' Earth in six days
And rested on th' seventh.
Same old story as we hear now:
Time limit set for labor
No matter whether the job's done er only half.
Now as I was sayin', not meanin' t' be sacrilligious,
I'm inclined t' think it might 'a' ben as well
If the Creator had worked another day mebbe
On this section o' V'mont
And leveled it off a little mite, in spots."

A Busy Day at the Scotsville Store

In spite of the bright sunshine,
Full of spring warmth, the March wind was raw.
There were still patches of snow on Danby Mountain
And folks said it would be cold until they were gone.
New wood smoke poured from the chimney of the small
   building
Where Simon Harrington kept his store.
He came out of the front door
And hurried to the shed on the end of the barn;
He jerked the shed door open and darted in.
In no time he was out again and headed for the woodpile.
He picked up an armful of newly sawed wood
And rushed back into the store.
More smoke poured from the overcrowded chimney.

Along towards noon Mis' Tabor came in.
She had her molasses jug in her hand.
Simon seemed a little annoyed at the intrusion
But he put the jug under the spigot.
A thin trickle emerged.
"It'll take a while, bein' so cold," Simon said.
He stood by the stove warming his hands a minute,
Then he darted out the front door.
Mis' Tabor had looked everything over in the store
And was watching from the window
When Simon came hurrying in.
He rushed to the back of the store.
The jug was standing in a crawling puddle of molasses.
Mis' Tabor heard Simon saying something.

14

He continued as he came out wiping the jug with some
    straw.
"My! my! my! Jest look at that! All over th' floor too."
He talked as fast as he could
And only paused when he ran out of breath.
"Th' cow's a-calvin', th' sheep's a-lambin'
Th' sow's a-piggin', and I got t' git me a clerk."
He set the jug on the floor.
"Th' price, Mis' Tabor, is twenty cents.
If you can lay down the right change
You won't have to wait fer me t' wash m' hands."

The Kelly Stand

Memories of the old days
Are often memories of a life that was hard;
The labors of the pioneers to clear the forest;
The struggle to wrest a living from the soil;
The isolation of mountain farms.

But the old tavern is holding fast to the gay days.
Perhaps its walls are weather-beaten and bulging;
And its piazza roof hangs down like a closed eyelid;
And its floors are rotting;
It's true that bricks strew the hearth
And the staircase is broken and shaky.

But under the sagging roof
The ballroom still stands,
With its arched ceiling clean and white.
The cracks in the plaster
Are only the wrinkles of old age.
The floor still springs as it used to do
When dancing feet made merry.

There, around the wall, are the built-in benches
Where tired dancers rested
After the final mad whirl of the Tempest.
There is the musicians' stand
With the long music rack across the front,
Where the four fiddlers drew their bows,
Stirring the blood of many a girl and swain.
Listen! Can't you hear the prompter's call,

Above the shuffle of the rhythmic steps,
And the mad surge of the singing fiddles?

Perhaps, there by the fan window,
You may see two lovers
Gazing off at the mountains—
Mountains tall, silent, enchanted
In the summer moonlight.

A rotting shell—the old tavern:
Full of ruin and decay,
While the carefree steps of dancing ghosts
Still echo through the arched ballroom.
They're dancing to the eerie music of the wind
In the dark spruces
By the fan window.

Deep Enough

Jake was one of those people
Who "somehow manage to get along."
He often referred to himself
As "Jackass at all trades."
He did seem to be able to find a way
To do many things demanding some amount of skill.
Now and then he thought of a way
That nobody else in the village had considered.
When his way worked he always made light of it
And nobody bothered to give him any credit.
Sam Loveland said Jake would spend a week
Rigging up something to save him an hour's work.
He'd managed to get well past middle age
And raise a small family
Without any help from the town.
In all his life he'd never had a steady job.
He had been the gravedigger for several years.
Digging each time for a new occupant
He didn't feel any tiresome sameness in that job.
Sam Loveland, however, found it necessary
To jack him up on the way he was doing his work.
"You're gettin' too all-fired slack," he said.
"You're diggin' these graves shallower and shallower.
If you can't keep 'em the proper deepness
I'll get somebody that can, that's all."
Jake pulled the end of his handle-bar mustache.
"Ain't heered of anybody gittin' out of 'em,
Hev yu?"

Roaring Branch Takes the Road

On either side of the winding road
The mountains cut the sky.
There were quick turns where the road
Clung to the rocky ledges of the mountain base,
Above the boulder-strewn bed of the brook.
In places the Branch had widened the valley
And there was a piece of new land
Where berry bushes made ready for the trees.
There the road rested from its climbing
And the brook was busy cutting the mountain
On the curve at the other side of the valley.
Then the climb began again.
The patch of sky grew wider as the mountains folded
    back.
The narrowing brook held truer to its course.
Then ahead the blue showed among the branches.

Now there is no road.
The brook, which years on years
Had cut its own highway to the river,
Has taken back its valley.
For days the cut-over slopes were beaten by rain.
Down each shallow gulley the water poured—
Down and down to join other torrents in wider gorges,
Until a mob of waters rolled ton boulders before it,
And ripped century-old trees from their rootholds,
Tossing them on the muddy foam like twigs.
It tore out the rock foundations of the road
And spread the gravel over the bush-grown flats.

Throwing spray high as it struck the final boulders,
It slipped out into the wide river valley,
There to loiter in a meadow,
Its strength all spent, its day of glory done.

Days after, men clambered up the brook-bed.
They stood and looked
And shook their heads.
The brook at last could have its valley.

Smuggler's Notch

The sign over the wide door read:
AUTO REPAIRING—GAS—OIL.
As the car slowed up by the gas pump,
The garageman hurried to the door and called,
"I'll be there'n a minute. Phone's a-ringin'."
The man in the car unfolded a map
And put it on the steering wheel.
He was showing his wife the route
When the garageman came out.
He put in the gas and came to the driver's seat.
The woman asked what mountain they had just come
    over,
And about the road going north to Canada.
"Ever been up through th' notch?" the garageman asked.
They hadn't. They asked if it was on their route.
He got on the running board and pointed on the map.
"Jest turn off below th' village here t' th' left
And cross the covered bridge. That'll take yu
Right up through Smuggler's Notch and back onto your
    rud."
They asked him if it was worth the extra miles.
He seemed shocked that anyone should ask such a ques-
    tion.
He went on to tell them the legend about the smugglers,
And about the mammoth spring and waterfall.
He spoke of the wildness of the country
And about the enormous boulders
On either side of the road.

He stopped and looked up the road.
"Yes," he spoke with reverence,
"There's them boulders lyin' all 'round
Jest as the Old Gent left 'em."

Noses

He had been known as WIMPY
Ever since he was a small boy.
His mother hadn't been quite sure in her speech
And WIMPY was as near as she could get to WILLIE.
Wimpy was through school long before he was finished.
In fact, he stopped going when he was of proper age.
He had stopped learning soon after he began.
Perhaps because the boys had bothered him,
He had grown into a man who kept to himself.
He had a few friends like the storekeeper
Who had always treated him with respect.
To such he often displayed unusual interests
Or a keenness of judgment that was startling.
To most people in the village
He was a harmless, sometimes pitiful, middle-aged man.
When he went to pick apples for Benjamin Barlow,
He found a man who treated him with kindness.
Mr. Barlow had known the family failings,
But he always made it a rule
To respect the dignity of the individual.
Out of friendly interest he asked Wimpy
About his mother and how his family was.
"I hear your sister got married recently."
(Mr. Barlow had heard of the fact
But the local gossip about it had escaped him.)
Wimpy didn't say anything while he reached for an apple.
He deposited it in the basket
And sat down on the top of the stepladder.
"Mr. Barlow, that brings t' mind

Suthin' my father used to tell me."
He blew his nose on a faded blue bandanna.
"He said there was three kinds of noses.
They was Roman noses, and Greek noses, and pug noses."
Wimpy stood up and started picking apples again.
"I couldn't never see that it made a mite o' difference
What kind of a nose a person had
Jest so he kep' it out of other folks' business."

Whose Democrat?

The Peasley place
Is just over the hill
South of the village.
James Peasley and his sister lived there
Until they were getting along in years.
Just when folks were wondering
How James could carry on the farm,
A city man, who'd spent the summer at the hotel,
Bought the place for a good round sum—
Enough so James and his sister
Could have lived in the village in some comfort.
They'd always had to save,
And they just couldn't spend with any comfort.
Of course, Jim didn't have any heavy work to do
And he did have time to rest when he was tired enough.
His sister never seemed to find time to rest.
She expected to do all of her resting later on.
One spring the man who had bought the Peasley place
Came up early to see about some improvements.
He found James cleaning up along his fence in the village.
He asked James how he and his sister had wintered,
And found they both wished they were back on the farm.
To change the subject he said:
"Well, I see Steve Older died."
"Yes, Steve passed away in January."
"So the Newfane Democrat's gone," the man continued.
"Yes, Steve's gone—but hold on!" James shifted his rake.
"He wa'n't the Newfane Democrat.
He lived jest over the line;
He was th' Dover Democrat."

June Comes to Tinmouth Valley

From the road the hill fell away to the valley.
There were fields marked off by bush-lined walls,
Warped barns, and weathered houses,
And twisting roads that made them neighbors;
Peaks of mountains banking another valley,
And the sharp wooded ridge that divided it from ours.
Above the road, green fields
Where the new grass, just grown high enough,
Bent to the soft sliding breeze.
Higher up the brown earth of a field just planted—
Rolled tight and smooth, and waiting.
And looking down on all the rest
The white farmhouse almost hidden by the maples.
Ahead the four points of the church tower
Pricked through the green leaves.
On the hill beyond, an old iron fence
Enclosed the rows of white stones.
Cloud shadows drifted across the fields.
A white throat sang three notes, stopped, and began again.
The wind brought the sound of running water.
The new leaves stirred—
Leaves only lately grown large enough
To give the wind a voice.
June had come to Tinmouth valley.

Big Business

Brayley came in from the back room
With a molasses jug in his hand.
He wiped around the cork with his finger
And licked the finger with signs of relish.
As he put the jug by the front door
Where old Quimby could get it,
A youngish man came up the steps.
He greeted Brayley uncertainly
Not quite sure whether he was a customer
Or the storekeeper.
Brayley enlightened him as briefly as possible
And went to his high desk at the back.
The young man followed.
Brayley gave no signs of hearing
But the young man went on with his story.
Finally he asked the storekeeper
If he didn't have a good many bad accounts.
Brayley guessed he had a few.
"Joining our credit rating agency, Mr. Brayley,
Would prevent all such losses."
Brayley looked past the young man.
"I got a credit agent o' m' own," he said.
The young man expressed surprise and some doubt.
Brayley crossed his legs and clasped his knee.
"Wal, y' see, I bought this store from Colonel Wetherbee.
He ain't got much to do sence he sold out,
So he sets there in that chair—well—
Consid'able o' th' time."
Brayley shifted legs and went on.

"First off I was fer trustin' everybody.
Then me an' th' Colonel fixed things up.
When a feller came in that wa'n't no good
The Colonel jest tapped twice onto th' floor with his
   cane."
Brayley turned to his books.
"So, yu see, young feller,
I ain't got no sort o' use fer what you're a-sellin'."

No Count

Miss Cole was a believer in "social security."
Not that such an expression had been heard then.
What she believed in was cutting her dress to fit the cloth.
She found herself, after her parents had passed on,
With a small comfortable house,
An acre or so of land around it,
And an income of three hundred dollars a year.
She also had fifty-odd years of living to her credit.
Her security came from managing her life
So that she had what she needed herself,
What she felt she should give to charity,
And a little to add to her savings bank account.
She had her own garden, of course,
And except for the plowing she cared for it.
That took care of much of her food.
She made jelly from her currants
And sold quite a bit of that for cash.
Then she had her chickens.
Somehow she had the ability to make them lay.
That brought in more cash, and food, too.
Each year she raised several lots of chicks.
Her days and part of her nights were given
To watching over her flocks,
From the time the first hen hatched her chicks.

She was moving rapidly around a small yard
In the middle of which a worried hen
Clucked to a scampering brood.
The parson stopped on his way to the post office.

29

"How many chickens in that brood, Miss Cole?"
Miss Cole turned quickly to head off an escaping chicken.
Without looking up, she said:
"Twelve. Then they's two that runs around so fast
I can't count 'em."

Cabe's Jewels

Cabe lived at the Poor Farm.
When he first drifted into town, sick,
He had to live there on the town
Or else he'd have died of exposure
And been buried at the town's expense.
That spring he made the old Poor Farm
Blossom like the rose.
When his flowers won prizes at the summer flower show
People began to ask him questions.
The next year he had plenty of work
And to the amazement of the town officers
That fall he insisted upon paying for his keep.
He stayed at the Farm because he liked the company.

Cabe had a weakness for jewelry.
He wore a long chain that had been his mother's
Around his neck, and on it a dollar watch.
On the side of his cap he had a glass-studded brooch,
And he always had a pin in his ragged necktie.

One morning he was working at the summer place of Dr.
  Higgins.
The Doctor noticed the brilliance of the stone
In a new pin Cabe had in his tie.
Cabe explained that he had picked it up on the road.
The Doctor looked it over and advised Cabe to advertise.
"That's a valuable stone and the owner would pay a good
  reward,"
He said, holding it where the stone caught the light.

Three weeks later Cabe was there again and he still had
the pin.
The Doctor spoke to him about finding the owner
Or, if he couldn't do that,
He advised him to sell it.
Cabe shook his head. "Nope, I sha'n't sell it," he said.
"Nobody came t' claim it from m' puttin' up a sign
Down to the post office neither."
"Oh, you did advertise it then?" The Doctor was re-
lieved.
Cabe leaned his spade against his hip
And spat on his hands.
"Yep, I hed a sign up fer three weeks—
But I writ it fine
And I posted it high."

The Right Thing but the Wrong Time

From the day when the colts were born
They assumed a place of importance
In the Blake family.
When father began to break them
They had become one of the serious concerns of life.
More thought, and perhaps effort, was expended
On bringing those roan colts up right
Than had been expended upon any of the children.
The first day father Blake, unaccompanied,
Drove them down the main street of the village
He felt it was his day of glory.

When the young son of the family
Was entrusted with the reins,
It was after weeks of coaching.
Then he was only allowed to drive them
When they were working on the farm.
Even that was honor enough for young William.
He heeded every admonition.
He took special care not to get them excited.
He never thought of leaving them unhitched.
It had been drilled into him
That if the colts should ever run away
They would be ruined for life.

One July day young William was driving the wagon
While his father loaded the hay onto the rack.
The hired man was raking after.
Father Blake went to the river bank

To gather up a tumble in a spot where the river curved.
Somehow he got too near the edge.
There was a loud splash and a muffled cry for help.
Young William in a frenzy stood on the hay rack
Yelling to the hired man to rescue his father.
As the man ran past he said in some wrath:
"Why don't ye go help 'im yerself stid o' standin' there?"
With a look of hopeless consternation the boy screamed:
"I want to! I want to! But how can I leave th' team?"

The Two Angels

When Henry Ranger had made his money,
He decided to spend it on improving himself.
He took a Cook's tour to Europe,
Being careful by habit to know the cost
Before he set sail.
He followed the itinerary to the letter.
Not once did he stay in his hotel
When the party was doing something improving.
He toured the galleries until his feet rebelled.

Among the things he brought home
Was a photograph of two marble angels.
He was especially taken with these statues
Because it had suddenly come to him
That he should do something for his home town.
He had always been on the board of managers of the
    cemetery
And he naturally thought of doing something for it.
The angels appeared on the horizon just then
And gradually a plan took shape.

The white angels, one on either gate post,
Had been in place for almost a week.
Not a soul had mentioned them to Henry.
He was puzzled and hurt.
He was looking at them with admiration,
When Jimmy Styles, the gravedigger, came out of the
    gate.

"Jimmy," Henry said, pointing to the two angels,
"How do folks in the village like those new statues?"
Jimmy glanced at the angels furtively,
"They don't mind 'em," he said, starting on.

Neighbors

Strangers often wondered about those two houses
Standing as close together as they could and not touch.
There was plenty of land in the village
And the other houses stood in the middle of the plots.
When you found out that these two neighbors
Hadn't spoken to one another for twenty-odd years,
You wondered even more that their houses almost
    touched.
Ed Bowser's house—the yellow one—stood
About in the center of the lot.
Jeremiah Lapham's lot hadn't a house on it then.
The two got into a row over the line
And Jeremiah lost the suit.
Then he went and built that house as close to the line
As he could possibly get it.
Then he rented it to a family with a lot of children.
Ed stood it for a while and then he built that addition
Just as close to Jeremiah's as he could and not trespass.
It cut all of the light off on that side of Jeremiah's house,
And it made things a little quieter for Ed
Because they never used the added rooms,
But it spoiled the looks of his place.
From time to time friends of both of them
Tried to make them give up their fight.
Neither one would make the first move.
Jeremiah died suddenly one spring
And the funeral was set for Sunday afternoon at the
    church.

37

One of the neighbors passed Ed going in the opposite
direction.

"Ain't yu goin' t' th' funeral?" he asked Ed.

Ed stopped short and looked at the speaker.

"No, I'm NOT going to the funeral."

He started on and then added over his shoulder:

"I'm heartily in favor of it though."

A Final Treat

Mrs. Judson had lived in the village
For almost twenty years.
She'd moved in from the hill road
When the farm was sold.
Her two sons and her one daughter
Would not hear of her living there alone
After her husband died.
He and she had given the best of their years
Getting a living off the rocky farm.
Besides that they had somehow scraped together
Enough money to educate all three children.
Mrs. Judson had never thought of money
As a thing one spent needlessly.
She "got along."
So it came about that when her two sons
Began sending small checks to her each month
She just didn't know what to do with the money.
What little she did spend
Was usually for the benefit of some neighbor.
She kept protesting when the checks came.
Finally she simply put them in the savings bank.

The youngest son was home for a week-end
And he was trying once more to persuade his mother
That there were things she really needed.
"What on earth is the use of saving the money?"
He said, almost losing patience.
"What are you going to do with it?"
His mother looked out of the window.

"Well, I'm saving it for my funeral," she said.
Her son looked at her with an affectionate twinkle.
"You just go and spend it, Ma.
I'll blow you to your last ride
When the time comes."

A Problem Solved

Probably few of the people in the valley
Ever knew what Wesley Forbes had gone through.
The younger generation knew he was an old man
Who lived alone in a four-room house,
And was reputed to be well-off.
A few of the older ones remembered.

Wesley was understood to have been a gold miner.
Sarah Pettus brought him to her farm,
When she came back from a visit to an uncle
Who lived in Montana:
They'd been married only a week then.
Wesley was a good worker, and it was a good farm;
He and Sarah seemed to get along well together.
Now and then Wesley would speak with longing
Of the free life of the West,
But that was only to a few of his cronies.

Soon after Sarah died, the neighbors were shocked
To see bills up announcing an auction.
Wesley sold everything off except a cow and a horse;
He did save a few chickens, too, and the old dog.
He moved down the road to the small house
Where the hired man had always lived.

He was telling about it a few years later:
"Livin' free like on the range,
I wan't never no hand at accumulatin' things.
I put up with it, livin' with Sary, 'cause I liked 'er."

He stopped a moment and then went on.
"When she went, all them things drove me crazy.
All to once I made up m' mind t' red me of 'em—
Gradual like till all's I hed left was th' old hoss."
He settled back in his chair and stuck his feet out.
"I got t' frettin' 'bout the old hoss one night.
Next mornin' I took m' gun and went out and shot the
    critter.
Sence then I got some peace livin'.
Life's full o' too tarnation many THINGS."

A Worrier

Ezra was really endowed
With a fairly rugged constitution.
He had been able at least to tend to the chores
For years without missing a day.
In spite of his evident good health,
Lamira, his wife, always looked after him
As though he were a fragile vessel.
If he came in with wet feet,
She insisted on dosing him to avoid a cold.
If he didn't eat his usual heavy meal,
She worried about his digestion.
She was forever running after him
To be sure he had enough on to keep warm.
He had become so used to it all
That he rarely lost his temper over it.

Then one fall he did have a real sick spell.
The doctor made him stay in bed for almost a week.
Lamira was nearly beside herself.
When he was up and about the house the first day
She watched his every move.
The next day when she was upstairs,
Ezra slipped into his boots and coat
And went out to the barn to see how things were.
He hadn't been there long before she came rushing out.
She made him come back to the chair by the stove.
By the time he was settled there
She had predicted everything but the last rites,
And she intimated that they might not be too remote.

When she'd done everything she could think of,
She started to go upstairs to finish her work.
"Now Ezry, you jest set there by that stove
Where yu belong.
If you don't do as you'd ought to,
I shall jest stop worrin' 'bout yu, that's all."

A Helpful Guardian

When the Colonel walked down the street
With his heavy cane in his hand,
He made quite an impression.
He was erect and well-built
And always careful about his dress.
His appearance and his deep, booming voice
Made strangers think he was domineering.
The people who knew him
Found that these were just outward trappings.
He was really a man of gentle spirit.

Jabez Hawks lived next to the Colonel.
He had a small vineyard back of his house.
On which he spent much time.
Every year when the grapes were ripe
Jabez had a war with the small boys of the village.
He made so much of this annual event
That the boys got more interested
In the battle than they were in the grapes.

One fall Jabez was called out of town
Just at the critical time.
He entrusted his grapes to the keeping
Of his neighbor the Colonel.
That evening the Colonel came on three boys
In the act of stealing some of the grapes.
He let loose on them with his booming voice,
Meanwhile brandishing his heavy cane.
He threatened them with immediate beatings

And subsequent arrest and incarceration.
Then, as they were retreating in terror, he called out:
"Say, if you boys had crept in at the back, there,
I wouldn't have known a thing about it."

Half Prepared

Morton Tupperton had left the village
When he was in his teens.
He'd clerked it for two years
In Brayley's store,
And then decided to get out into the world.
Folks said he was foolish to leave a steady job
Just on the say-so of a "runner" for a New York house.
Members of the traveling profession
Were usually looked on askance
By the people in the village.
There was something mysterious about them.

It was only two years later that Morton himself
Was a "runner" for the same house.
He had a section out West for his territory
So he didn't get back to the village.
Now and then some of his relatives heard from him,
And as time went on he sent them presents.
People's ideas of him underwent a change.
He seemed to be amounting to something.

He'd been a partner in his firm for some ten years
When the New York paper announced his death.
Later the village was aghast at the fortune
Which reports stated Morton had left.
A large sum was willed to a museum.
Ed Brayley was reading about it in the morning paper.
"I see it says it's t' be spent fer a wing,
T' be knowed as th' TUPPERTON WING.

47

By gosh!"

Old man Sitwell listened with his hand behind his ear. "A wing?" he asked in a voice that always trembled, "Wal, mebbe he thought he'd be sure o' one anyhow."

The Gamble of Matrimony

The first change Uncle Ezra noticed
In his young nephew was a tendency to dream.
He'd come on him several times
Sitting under a tree gazing into space.
Then one evening, right in the middle of the week,
He appeared after supper in his Sunday clothes.
He was gone from the room
Before Uncle Ezra had a chance to speak.
Uncle Ezra sat there with his paper in his lap,
Looking over his glasses at the hurrying figure.
In a few minutes the nephew drove past the window
With the driving horse hitched to the new buggy.
Uncle Ezra didn't get much information
When he spoke about the matter the next morning.
"I just went t' th' village," the nephew said.

By late summer Uncle Ezra's calendar
Was all mixed up by his nephew's strange doings.
The sacred rites of Saturday night
And the clothing of the Sabbath
Became parts of almost any evening.
By then Uncle Ezra knew it was love.
He also knew who the girl was.
That meant he knew her entire pedigree
Back to the first settlements in the valley.
As a bachelor of many years' standing,
Uncle Ezra had a certain disdainful attitude
Which he felt he must maintain.
Inwardly he was getting a vicarious joy out of it.

A few days before the wedding,
The nephew came in from the field
And sat down to rest on the back porch.
Uncle Ezra sat there in his chair
Shelling peas for dinner.
Without looking up from his pea shelling, he said:
"When a woman gets married she's a cocoon.
They ain't no way o' tellin'
Whether she'll turn out a butterfly
Er a snappin' bug."
He reached for another handful of peas.

The Lawyer

Probably, up to the time Ed came along,
No member of the Grooper family
Had received a formal education
Beyond what is now the fourth grade.
Ed's father could read, though he rarely did,
And his writing was confined to signing his name.
Ed was the youngest of the Grooper children.
His three sisters and two brothers
Had shown no more interest in their books
Than tradition called for.
Ed was entirely different.
He was careful of his dress from early youth
And he scorned even the few manual chores
Which had been demanded of the others.
Being the youngest he was honored.
When he showed aptitude at school
His father was proud as he could be.
He decided Ed should be somebody.
When, at the age of fourteen,
Ed told a waiting world he would be a lawyer,
His father's pride knew no bounds.

When Ed had finished high school with some honor,
He went at once to the law office of Henry Stickles.
Mr. Stickles had taken an interest in Ed
Because Ed's father did his gardening.
So Ed's father was always talking about
"My son Ed, the lawyer."

No matter what the subject of conversation might be
Somehow he'd bring Ed in.

When the census-taker came to the Grooper house
He asked Tom Grooper about his family.
"Well, sir," Tom said, as he removed his pipe,
"There's the three girls,
And the two boys,
And my son Ed, the lawyer."

A Real Day's Work

While Joel was washing up at the sink,
Miss Meeker was getting the dinner on the table.
As he was putting his cuffs on,
She was testing a cake on the oven ledge
With a piece of broom straw.
Then they adjourned to the dining-room.
When Joel had satisfied the first pangs of hunger,
He asked Miss Meeker about her brother.
"Since I moved over t' other side th' river,
I sorta lost track o' m' old neighbors.
Never thought 'twas so near dinner-time though."
He added the last remark as a continuation of an apology.
He'd been assuring Miss Meeker, ever since he'd come,
That he had no intention of staying for a meal.
Miss Meeker shoved her plate away
And put her elbows on the table.
"Well, Ab isn't real rugged.
You know he sold his farm and lives here with me."
Joel, busy with food, murmured: "You don't tell me."
"Oh, yes, his heart got so bad the doctor made him sell
    out.
He can't do much now except chorin' around most of the
    time.
He manages to get in a fair day's work but nothin' heavy.
Can't do any fine work since a cataract come on his other
    eye."
Miss Meeker paused to pour out some tea.
"Then bein' crippled some with rheumatiz in his hands
It keeps him from doin' lots o' things.

The doctor said when he'd had what teeth he had pulled
His stomach trouble'd let up.
Seem's though it was worse.
He don't eat skurse anythin'."
Joel, still busy with his plate, murmured sympathy.
"No, he's drove down to the village t'day
T' see about some medicine he read a piece about in th'
   paper.
Makes it kinda hard on me in th' summer
When I have a house full o' city boarders.
Take it all in all, and that lame foot o' his,
He don't make out t' do a real day's work."
She sighed and poured out another cup of tea.

Better Than Credit

It was back in the days
When "F.H." ran the village store.
Of course, he was a hotelman
But at various times he took over
Other lines of business for short periods.
He'd been running the store for some months
When he found his manager
Had let Henry Sawyer run up quite a bill.
"F.H." called his attention to it
And told him not to let him have anything more
Until he'd paid up.
In spite of his orders,
Somehow Henry managed to buy more on credit.
"F.H." said a few things in his decided way
And the manager agreed to put a stop to Henry.

The following Saturday "F.H." met Henry on the street.
Henry had his arms full of groceries.
"F.H." stopped him.
He looked at him with a withering glance,
Which didn't bother Henry at all.
"Henry," "F.H." said, "where'ju get those things?"
Henry shifted his packages.
"Down to your store," he said.
"Did you pay for 'em?"
Henry looked defiant.
"Nope. I had 'em booked."
"F.H." looked straight at Henry for a minute.
"Henry, I'll make a bargain with yu.

If you'll agree never to go to my store again,
I'll cross off what you've got on the books
And give you what you've got there now."
Henry hesitated. Then he said,
"Guess not, 'F.H.,'
I think I kin do better 'n that."

The Lord on His Side

Maria Templeton had always bossed her husband.
What she couldn't achieve by mastery she accomplished
  by nagging.
When she decided to get rid of the old barn she struck
  a snag.
It stood at the edge of the lower meadow.
It hadn't been used for years except for surplus hay
And each year its roof sagged more,
And its weather-beaten sides bulged to the bursting point.
Every time Maria looked from her kitchen window
The old barn roused her anger.

One bleak November day, when the barn added to the
  darkness,
Maria decided the time for action had come.
She told her husband she wanted it torn down.
"Well, now, seem's most too good t' tear down," he said.
She turned from the window.
"Then give it to somebody for taking it away."
William shook his head.
"Well, now, I ain't sure it cud be moved."
Maria snorted and cited movings of big houses in the
  village.
"Yes . . . but . . ."
"There ain't any and, if, er but about it," Maria insisted,
"That barn is goin' somehow."

A few days later Maria informed William
That Joel Tomkins had agreed to remove the barn

Just as soon as the ground was frozen.
He could use it on his place.
William blinked and said nothing.

When the ground froze and snow came,
Joel had work carpentering in the village.
"Sorry, Mis' Templeton, but I need th' cash," he told
Maria.
When the spring thaws came there the old barn stood
Looking worse than ever at the edge of the sodden
meadow.

In May the barn was still there.
Maria's patience was about exhausted.
"Why on earth don't he move it stead o' jest comin' and
lookin' at it!"

William was telling the storekeeper about it.
"Y' see Maria ain't run up agin anybody she couldn't boss
afore."
The storekeeper looked over his spectacles.
"I didn't know as Joel was so set in his way," he said.
"Gad! He ain't. He's been ready sence snow went.
It ain't Joel. It's the *Lord*.
He set three springs into that lower medder."

Seeing's Not Believing

There was a good attendance at the store.
The biting north wind made a fair excuse
To let the woodpile go for a while
And sit close to Brayley's chunk stove.
The two chairs were occupied and the bench
Made of a board set on two kegs of nails.
Even the counter was occupied except in the rare intervals
When a real customer happened to come in.
The temperature records had been gone over
With Grandpa Bull having the last say.
He always reported several degrees lower than anybody
    else
And, as he always kept records in a diary,
His reports were usually taken as final.
Job Stillson brought the news
That the Barrows boy had set up a windmill on his fence.
"By cricky, that feller's a heller, whittlin'."
Job lifted his cap to uncover his ears.
"I'll be gol darned if this ain't a double contraption
With a little mill on top of a bigger one."
Grandpa Bull opined there "wa'n't nothin' onusual 'bout
    that,"
And went on to tell about one he'd seen when he was
    young.
"But this cussed thing's different," Job insisted.
"The top one goes one way and the bottom one t'other."
Job found his audience skeptical,
And Grandpa Bull said, "It just ain't possible, that's all."

At noon Grandpa went home by way of the Barrows house.

The Barrows boy came along and found him

Gazing at the two mills, one going one way, the other another.

As Grandpa started on, the boy heard him say,

"Well, by hellum, I don't believe it!"

A Lender

The auctioneer stood by the back door
On the marble step with a slanting trough in the center
Made by three generations of heavy-shod farmers.
On the porch, chairs were piled with small things
To be offered in lots before the crowd had warmed up.
Men were bringing things out from the kitchen,
To be ready as the sale went on.
People were wandering around the house
Looking over the bigger pieces of furniture.
What had been for almost a hundred years a home
Had, since breakfast that morning,
Become a second-hand store open to all comers.
The voice of the auctioneer grew stronger
As the bidding became more active.
By noon the auctioneer had moved to the barn
Where the men had been dragging out the farm machin-
    ery.
Wagons, harnesses, plows, hay rakes, were put up.
Finally, the auctioneer turned to a rusty mowing machine.
He called for bids, making a joking remark
About the antique value of this machine.
Samuel Giddings raised it a quarter.
Sam's son edged up to his father.
"You don't want that, Pa. What yu thinkin' of!"
The bid was raised and Sam went to one-fifty.
"What in time do yu want o' that piece of junk?"
Sam's son went on. "We got a good machine now."
"Once, twice— Yu all done? Sold to Sam Giddin's."

Sam turned to his disgusted son,
"Keep yer mouth shut, will yu! I know what I'm
  doin'.
I'm gittin' this one t' lend t' the neighbors."

Help in Need

It was his last Saturday in the valley.
He had come to the village church,
Two years before, fresh from the Seminary.
As he walked along the road he remembered
How many Saturday evenings he had followed it,
Going, as he was now, to see Mrs. Camden.
He'd been called there soon after he'd come to the val-
    ley,
When her husband had been hurt in the haymow.
He'd been impressed with her quiet efficiency.
During the two years no family in the valley
Had suffered so many misfortunes.
Crops had been bad,
The barn had burned with much of the stock.
Then, only a few weeks ago, Mrs. Camden had fallen
And broken her shoulder.

The young minister stopped in front of the house.
Once again he got the view of the quiet valley,
With the mountains beyond stretching north and south,
With one high peak reaching into the sky.

He had been telling Mrs. Camden
How she had been an inspiration to him—
Her steadfast courage and quiet acceptance,
No matter what hard things came her way.
"I wonder, Mrs. Camden, if you would tell me
What verse of Scripture you have found most helpful."

63

Mrs. Camden shifted the bandaged shoulder.
"Well, Parson," she said after some hesitation,
"I reckon I've got the most help
Out of 'Grin and bear it.'"

An Unfortunate Break

When Hattie Wilkins married Zed Howe
Nobody in the village understood it.
Hattie was full of energy.
She had taught school for several years
And carried on her mother's small place
At the same time.
It was two years after her mother died
That she married Zed
And went to live on his neglected farm.
Zed had always been shiftless.
He was strong on talking
But weak when it came to putting his theories
Into practice on his own fertile acres.

Hattie, with the help of a good hired man,
Brought the farm back to usefulness.
In summer she took boarders
And Zed spent much of his time
Telling them about agriculture.
He exasperated Hattie almost beyond endurance
But she managed to get him to go for the boarders
When they arrived at the train,
And to make regular trips to the village.
These usually took longer than necessary.
One afternoon, when Hattie was rushed in the kitchen
Preparing supper for a houseful of boarders,
The hired man came in, out of breath and excited.
He reported that Zed had fallen from the haymow

And broken his leg.
Disgusted, Hattie hurried out to the barn.

She was telling about it later.
"There he set, groanin',
And not a chore done ner even started."
She stirred something in a kettle vigorously.
"If it wan't jest like 'im,
And me with a houseful of boarders!"

South Londonderry Air

On that road that goes over the hill
Between North and South Londonderry
There used to be a thriving settlement known as MIDDLE-
  TOWN.
There was a church and the schoolhouse and the "hearse
  house."
That was when the town furnished the conveyance
For the citizen's last ride, usually behind the family team.
Some people remember, when they were younger,
How spooky the black hearse used to look in its house
When they climbed a slanting tree to peek through the
  window.
As usual the valley with its mills along the streams
Gradually drew the people from the hills.
They even moved the church down from Middletown.
Now it's part of a garage in the village.
That large house on the left
Belonged to old Doc Collins years ago.
His two children lived there—
Emeline, an old maid, and Henry, an old bachelor.
Henry carried on the farm with the help of Nelson Clark.
Nelson wasn't always a help.
He was strong and a good worker
But his mental equipment was decidedly lacking.
One day Henry wanted to send Nelson to the village
And he told him to go and saddle the horse.
When Henry came out to tell Nelson what to do at the
  village
He found him waiting with the horse by the back door.

He started to speak and then stopped.
"Nelson," he said in his usual drawl,
"You've got that saddle on back side to."
Nelson looked at the saddle.
A crafty look came on his face as he said:
"Mebbe you don't know which way I'm goin'."

Economics

The talk around the village
Was centered in the coming Town Meeting.
The town report had been gone over at the store
And any town officer who was not present
Had come in for considerable criticism.
The few officers who happened to be around the stove
Were only too glad to direct attention from themselves.
One thing was conspicuously absent—
Not a word of praise was offered for anyone.
Silence about himself was the nearest to praise a man got.
There was a good deal of interest in the candidate for
    lister
Because it was the year for the quadrennial appraisal.
Almost to a man each voter in Brayley's store
Felt *his* property was in too high,
And without any trouble they picked out others
Who should have *their* property listed higher.
Gradually they worked around to a discussion
As to how the value of real estate could be determined.
Finally, Hen Loveland, who had been smoking and lis-
    tening,
Tapped his pipe on the stove and stood up.
"Speakin' of figgerin' what things is wuth.
I recollect old man Filley had a litter o' pigs.
'How much are you figgerin' them pigs'll be wuth
Come spring?' a neighbor asked Filley.
'Wall, I figger they'll be wuth
All the little fellers'll fetch,' says Filley."

The Irrepressible Truth

Jared Sanford had peddled milk in the village
Ever since enough people had given up
Keeping their own cows to make a milk route pay.
There had been some who had held out
Because they had a pet cow,
Or because they had plenty of free pasturage
And just couldn't see any reason for paying out money
For something they had always raised themselves.
Jared was one who looked out for any chance
To get in a little extra cash.
He had begun by supplying a few neighbors
With his surplus milk;
Gradually he had driven out the others
Who were doing the same thing.
People might complain about the quality,
Or worry about the dirt in the bottom of the pitcher,
But Jared always had a good excuse ready.
Sometimes, as the result of such complaints,
There would be more cream in the milk for a few days.

Jared's son Thomas was twelve years old
When his father began to let him help with the route.
Thomas was long and lanky, with honest blue eyes;
He took the milk business very seriously.
One morning Jared found so much on hand to do at home
That he sent Thomas out alone.
Sam Elder was standing at his gate that morning
When the young milkman came along.
Sam greeted him warmly:

"Well, Thomas," he said, smiling,
"How much water'd your father put in the milk this
   morning?"
Young Thomas looked troubled for a minute;
Then his face cleared:
"He only put in a little, Mr. Elder.
He said it wan't enough to do a mite o' harm."

A Vermont Guidepost

Somehow that turn to the right
Always seemed to be taking the traveler
Away from Skowhegan,
In spite of the fact that it really led there.
This time a passenger was especially skeptical—
Taking that road somehow seemed against nature.

Right at the turn there was a farm
And sitting on a hayrack was the farmer,
Either asleep or deep in thought.
A boy was puttering around near the road;
He appeared startled by the request for information
As to the proper route to Skowhegan
And called to Pa to "Come 'ere."
Pa came to life at once;
He jumped from the hayrack and approached the car.
He was tall, thin, straight, and bright-eyed.
Bristly whiskers, not unlike the uncut grass
In the meadow across the road, covered his face.
He acknowledged the greeting with a nod,
And lifted one foot to the running board
As he leaned toward the speaker in the car.
"Is this the road to Skowhegan?"
He shoved his hat back and looked up the road.
"Well, you can go that way."
"What's the best way?"
Again the farmer shifted his hat.
"The way you're goin'," he said.
Taking his foot from the running board he walked away.

Only Two Faults

Samuel leaned against the fence
And let the breeze blow through his sweat-soaked shirt;
His face was red and his hair was wet.
A bay mare was tied to a post beside him;
She also showed signs of exertion.
Being a horse-trader as well as a farmer,
Samuel was used to all kinds of horse-flesh
And he had been learning that this bay mare,
Once she was let loose, was far from easy to catch.
He'd traded for her two days before
And turned her out to pasture.
As he fanned himself with his broad-brimmed straw,
He decided the bay mare shouldn't stay there long.
Just then Newt Lovell drove into the yard.
Newt came from up the valley;
He did little with horses but he had a cash customer
Who wanted a light driving horse.
He didn't let it be known just what he was after
And Samuel talked about every horse he had but the
    mare;
However, he had seen Newt look at her when he drove
    in.
Finally, Newt asked about the mare
And Samuel told him she wasn't anything he wanted.
Then Newt talked of something else, but came back to
    the mare.
Samuel told him she had a "couple o' outs."
Newt looked her over with an inexperienced eye.
"What's wrong with 'er? I can't see nothin'."

Samuel hooked his elbows over the fence board,
"She's awful hard t' catch. Wore me all out this morn-
in'."
Newt didn't think that was so bad.
He finally offered "one and a half."
Samuel, delighted at the offer, appeared indifferent.
After more talk he reluctantly accepted.
When the trade had been concluded Newt said:
"You said she had a couple o' outs. What's th' other?"
Samuel handed him the halter rope.
"Well, 's I said, she's hard t' catch.
Only other thing I know of,
She ain't worth a damn after you've ketched 'er."

Winter Draws Near

The grass was still green in the meadow
Where the cattle had been turned in
To do their last cropping
Before the winter diet of stored hay, grain, and fodder.
The barns were bulging, and near by two haystacks
Stood out against the sky as the sun sank beyond the hill.
Brown patches on the wooded slopes
Marked the stands of oak.
The open door of the shed showed squared ends
Of dry maple piled to the ceiling.
In the corner there was a pile of knotty chunks
Filled with waiting warmth for winter fires.

Ed came out of the cellar door
With a basket on his arm.
Down there the potato bin was full;
There were things buried in the sand;
And others covered deep in straw.
On the shelves, row on row of last summer's garden
    surplus
Stood in glass jars, beside the jelly and conserves.
The big crocks in the corner were waiting for the pork,
Still grunting out behind the barn.

As the quick autumn twilight stole the daylight,
Ed went in through the shed to the kitchen;
He took off his boots and his jumper
And washed at the sink.
As he sat down by the stove to wait for supper,

Mrs. Ed handed him a letter.

"I hope that brother of yours isn't having more trouble,"
She said, having noted the name on the envelope.
Ed read in silence for a few minutes:
"Well, he's worried about the stock market,
And the prices of food in the city are awful."
He turned the page and smiled.
"Says he had t' get a new heater. Bedrooms wouldn't
heat."
Mrs. Ed stirred something on the stove.
"That reminds me, I moved into the downstairs bedroom
today.
Guess I better open the door and let it get nice and
warm."
Ed folded up the letter and put it back in the envelope.
"'Twas gettin' chilly upstairs, and it's goin' t' be cold
t'night.
Mebbe you'd better put a stun in the oven, too."

Under the Spreading Chestnut Tree

In the days when a blacksmith
Could make a good living just shoeing horses,
Ned Witten had all of the business he could handle.
He had a way with horses with a nasty temper—
He always kept one of that kind to drive himself—
And some of his customers came from other towns
Because of his reputation.
He was large in frame but he spoke softly;
Many a time he would quiet a horse shaking with fear
By talking to it and laying a reassuring hand on its flank.

As horses grew scarce Ned took on automobile work;
He got into it gradually and with some distaste.
Even when there was not enough shoeing to say so
He kept his forge and his anvil ready.

The car came to a stop by the door,
And the driver opened the window.
"Can you do some work on this car?
You do automobile work, don't you?"
Ned went to the door, his hands under his leather apron.
"Yes, sir. I can fix yer car.
I do anythin' from hoss shoein' "—
He paused—
"Down."

Each to His Last

Ezra Bump was driving along the back road
That goes over the hill to the Dent place.
It's one of those roads that seems to dread the climb.
It dallies along the brook, first one side and then the
other.
Then, when it gets to where it can't escape the hill,
It rushes straight up without even a turn to ease the
climb.
Ezra was letting his horse take its time,
Being in no more hurry than the road to get over the
crest.
Around the last bend before the climb
He came on the two city men who were boarding at the
Stiles'.
He'd passed the time of day with them the day before.
They stopped to let him pass but Ezra drew up beside
them.
"What you fellers doin' t'day?"
Ezra turned so his feet hung over the wheel.
The men seemed surprised but admitted they had noth-
ing on hand.
"Well, now," Ezra went on, "you know, er mebbe yu
don't,
Old Man Dent died this spring. He lived over th' ridge."
Ezra nodded toward the west.
"Th' Widder's got a lot o' hay down
And nothin' in th' way o' help but a hired hand.
I'm goin' over and I thought you fellers mebbe
Might be needin' a mite o' exercise."

One of the strangers had done haying in his boyhood;
The other had never had a hay fork in his hand.
After a minute's hesitation they agreed to drive over
And give Ezra a lift with the hay.

The first load was on the rack.
Ezra wound the reins around his fork
And pulled a plug of tobacco from his pocket.
The two helpers were wiping their dripping faces.
They felt they had made a good showing
Even if the hired man, alone on his side of the load,
Had kept up with the two of them.
Ezra got his chew limbered up.
"What you fellers do fer a livin' down to th' city?"
The one who had never hayed it before leaned on his
    fork;
He was feeling quite pleased with his efforts.
"Oh, I spend my time at a desk figuring insurance rates."
Ezra unwound the reins and braced his feet.
Over the side of the load, he said:
"Well, I don't s'pose I'd be any better at that
Than you be at pitchin' on hay."

Givers

Sarah Dunlap was probably the largest giver
Living in the village.
She was also as little endowed with worldly goods
As anyone in the valley.
Of all the people there she was the only one
Who knew what it meant to give until it hurt.
She couldn't give anything without missing it.
Because she was always cheerful and ready to help,
Most people took her kindness as a matter of course.
It never seemed to be any trouble for her
To stay with a sick neighbor.
She was usually the last one out of the kitchen
After a church supper;
She always took the dish towels home to wash.
Sid Covey was talking about her in the store one evening.
Perhaps he was led to especial praise
By the uncharitable countenance of Deacon Tightwell.
The Deacon looked on whatever giving he did as an investment.
He never gave unless he was sure of a return.
What he put on the plate was supposed to return to him
In esteem from those who saw him drop his dutiful coin.
(This was somewhat lessened as an investment when the treasurer
Reported that the Deacon must have a hoard of three-cent pieces.)
Finally, Sid's comments stirred the Deacon to remark
That it was more blessed to give than to receive.
He warmed to his subject and closed with a plea

That they should all give to the support of missions
And "give until it hurt."
Sid listened until the Deacon was through.
"Give till it hurts, eh?
By gosh, they's some that suffers agonizin' pain
Jest from th' thought o' givin'."

Time Isn't Money

Ever since Mrs. Newcomer had bought the Bligh place
And become a resident of the village
She had had a help problem.
By "help" she meant a servant.
She gave the orders and they were to be obeyed.
When she tried that on the natives
She found they wished to help, but in their own way.
They felt they were hired to do what she wanted done
In a way that they themselves thought best.
They were not used to taking orders either.
They might be told what Mrs. Newcomer would *like*
    done,
But they wouldn't stand being told flatly to do this or
    that.
Willie Wellman stayed longer than anybody else.
He was very deaf and had little to say.
Mrs. Newcomer simply wrote him her orders
And he usually carried them out.
At least he got something like the results she expected.
Best of all Willie didn't stop to visit;
The others always leaned on their hoe or the lawnmower
Whenever she or anyone else came near enough for con-
    versation.
Alonzo Corbitt quit because this right was curtailed.

He was mowing the front lawn when somebody came
    along.
Mrs. Newcomer looked out to see Alonzo

Leaning on the mower and talking earnestly with the
   stranger.
She went out on the porch and moved the chairs,
Then she stood and stared at Alonzo;
He kept right on talking.
When the man had left she went out.
She finished her tirade with:
"And here I am paying you good money
And you stand there and visit!"
Alonzo dropped the mower handle
And started toward the tree where his coat lay.
"Nope, Mis' Newcomer. You ain't payin' me nothin'."

Butter

Old man Ellery used to say
That "Mis' Penny was expectin' an awful wet spell."
Her preparations for a rainy day were proverbial.
When she was asked to provide for a church supper,
The Ladies' Aid knew that the answering cake
Would cause no digestive disturbances from richness.
Milton, her husband, never asked for her dishes
As many a husband did for his own wife's specialties.
He managed to stow away much more at such public
   feasts
Than his gaunt figure would seem to demand.
The fact was he never had enough to eat at home.
His wife was much more interested
In fattening the account in the savings bank.
It was to add to it that she consented
To "take" the young lawyer who had moved to town.
Of course, she didn't run a boarding house
But she did now and then "take" somebody.
The young lawyer was settled there
Before anyone had a chance to warn him.
He was especially fond of butter—
A commodity which Mis' Penny considered a luxury.
She had it on her table but neither she nor Milt
Used it in more than homeopathic doses.
The young lawyer shocked her the first day
By spreading it generously on his bread.
He even used it to give some flavor
To the very pale doughnuts he had at breakfast.
Mis' Penny said nothing for a few days.

Finally, she could restrain herself no longer.

"Butter's awful high," she said at supper.

"It costs fifty cents a pound."

Her boarder helped himself to another generous slab.

As he spread it on his bread, he replied:

"Well, I should say it was well worth it."

A Boat Trip

Even when Hosea was a young man
It was reported that to fit him to pants
All they had to do was to measure a molasses cask.
He was active in spite of his size
And usually led off in the dances in the Grange Hall.
His fancy steps were a thing to watch.
Toward middle age
He got too stiff in the joints to dance.
By the time he was sixty he was just able to hobble
With the help of two canes.
The town paid Martha Starkweather to board Hosea.
When he got so he couldn't move from his room
She took good care of him.
Then one morning she found her boarder had died in his
    sleep.
When the selectmen went to arrange for Hosea's funeral
The undertaker told them he hadn't a coffin big enough.
They found that Peter Stiles, the carpenter,
Was visiting his sister over the mountain.
That was how the Captain happened to build Hosea's
    coffin.
He had only moved to the village a year before;
He had been a sailor most of his life
And knew how to build boats.
So the selectmen asked him to make a coffin for Hosea.
He said he'd never done such a job,
But if he could build a boat that would sail
He ought to be able to build a coffin that would fit.

It was noon of the day of the funeral
When the selectmen heard he had the coffin done.
They sent the undertaker over with his wagon to get it.
He found the Captain standing by the coffin scratching
  his head.
"Yep, she's done, and done ship-shape," he said.
"But dinged if I ain't got a center-board in 'er."
The undertaker looked it over.
"Well," he said, taking hold of one end,
"I reckon it'll hold Hosea,
And mebbe with that center-board
He'll hev an easier trip across th' river."

After the Storm

Job Atkins was looking over his meadow.
The brook, swollen by the fall rains,
Had gone on a rampage.
Over in one corner of the meadow
It had spread a mat of silt and rocks,
Spoiling perhaps two acres of good land.
Along the roadside several old elms
Lay on the stone wall, their roots sticking up.
Judson Purdy came toward him on the road.
He had a cross-cut saw in his hand.
"Been clearin' the rud down th' hill," he said, drawing
    near.
"I never see such a tangle o' toppled trees."
Job leaned his back against the fence.
"Kinda pickin' on us, seem's though,
Flood and wind all t' once.
Noah only had th' flood.
Do any damage t' your place?"
Judson leaned on his saw.
"No, nothin' to speak of.
Water did a mite o' cuttin' back th' house.
Then th' wind blew m' hog pen clean over th' fence."
Job whistled: "Wheeuw!"
"I didn't know nothin' of it till mornin'.
I went down t' feed th' stock;
Th' hog pen wan't to be seen,
And there set that durned hog
Madder'n hell."
"Can't say as I blame 'im," Job said.

A Hired Man

Old Joe had worked on most of the farms
Up and down the valley.
Sometimes he would stay several years at a place;
Then he'd get sick of his surroundings and go off.
Nobody knew much about his past
And Joe never added to their knowledge.
In spite of all he could do to hide it
He had good blood in his veins.
Wherever he worked he was welcome in the family;
He was neat and quiet in the house
And he was very fond of children.
He usually broke over at fair-time in the fall.
No matter how pressing the work
He'd throw up his job and go to all the fairs
Within fifty miles of the village.
He'd spend every cent he had saved during the year
On the races and on liquor.

One time he'd given up a two years' job
And had his annual fling at the fairs.
He had caught a ride back with one of the Powers boys.
When they stopped at the watering trough by Ned Pike's
  place
Ned paused on his way to the barn
And asked Joe what he was doing.
Joe said he wasn't doing anything.
"Well, why can't yu come help me tomorrer?
I'm awful back with m' fall work."
Joe said he guessed he could

And agreed to be on hand the next morning.
A mile or so further on Nate Penfield stopped him;
He was short of help and wanted Joe's assistance.
Joe agreed to be on hand the next morning at seven.
As they drove away the Powers boy told Joe
What he thought of such conduct.
"Here you go and agree t' be in two places
Tomorrow mornin' at seven o'clock.
They'll both be plannin' on havin' you, too.
'Tain't right, Joe."
Joe looked down at the dashboard.
"Won't only one of 'em be disappointed," he said.
The Powers boy slapped the horse with the reins.
"But that ain't doin' right by him.
Which one's goin' t' be disappointed, anyhow?"
Old Joe recrossed his legs and settled down on the seat.
"Whichever feller I go t' work for, I guess."

Winter Comes to Tinmouth Valley

The road wound through the winter woods
Where the shadows of trees lay on the smooth snow.
It dipped down to a small brook
With frost-covered bushes leaning over it.
Uneven stone walls, partly buried in drifts,
Followed it on either side up the hill.
The woods ended and there was the valley,
A white sheet a mile wide, sagging in the middle,
Pinned to the sides of the mountains by scattered trees,
Up to the dark line of spruce and pine.
Then beside the road winding across the valley
Barns and houses emerged.
Clean wood smoke, that made a gray curling shadow on
    the snow,
Rose straight up from kitchen chimneys.
In barnyards cattle stood on the sunny side,
Or crowded by the stable door waiting for milking time.
Some sheep nibbled hay from a fenced-in stack
Which cast a hive-shaped shadow on the snow.
Across a white field a team drew a load of logs.
Steam rose from the panting horses.
A dog ran back and forth in front of them.
The tinkle of their bells came on the crisp air.
The black fence around the white stones stood out on its
    hill,
The stones uneven spots in the smooth covering.
The shadow of the west mountains drew a black line.
It slid slowly across the valley.
The sheep crowded together by the haystack.

The cattle marched in solemn line into the warm barn.
Along the slopes of the eastern mountains
The purple shadow crept up to the last lilac light on the
  highest peak—
Hovering cold, and waiting silence.
Winter night had come to Tinmouth valley.

A Helper

It was getting dark when Dr. Richards came in.
He had fed his tired horses and bedded them.
For ten days he'd been struggling through drifts
To get to some of his snow-bound patients.
Often he had to tie his horse to a tree
And go the last mile or so on snowshoes.
As he went toward the house he noticed it was snowing
   again.
The wind was rising, too. He could hear it on the moun-
   tain.
As he finished his supper, he was telling his wife
How worn out his two horses were.
Just then the phone rang.
It was a relayed call from the lumber camp
Seven miles back on the mountain.
Neither the doctor nor his wife questioned his going.
It was the tired horses he thought of.
Then he remembered that Ed Hinton had said
That he'd be glad to take him on some of his calls.
He could work his bill down that way.
Ed was husky and he had boasted about his horses.

They had made the camp in good time,
In spite of the fast-falling drifted snow.
The cracked harness had broken once
But the doctor had mended it with a snowshoe thong.

The crushed foot had demanded careful attention
And it was late when Dr. Richards and Ed

Started back down the mountain.
New drifts had piled up in the road.
The bitter wind drove the swirling snow before it.
Ed began to wonder if they shouldn't turn back.
The harness broke again and the doctor mended it
While Ed stood huddled in his sheep-lined coat.
Near the foot of the mountain the tired horse,
Struggling through a drift, lost his footing.
He sank down in the snow, worn out with the struggle.
"Guess we're in fer it, Doc," Ed said hopelessly.
The doctor was busy freeing the horse from the sled.
Both of the brittle thills had snapped.
"Here, take hold," he said to Ed.
"We'll leave the sled in the bushes here."

The doctor's wife went to the window for the hundredth
    time.
She was turning away again
When she thought she saw something moving.
She rushed to open the kitchen door.
The doctor, his coat plastered with snow,
Emerged from the swirling cloud.
He was leading the drooping horse.
Behind them came Ed, only his hat showing above his
    collar.

As Ed was leaving for home after some hot coffee,
Mrs. Richards said: "Ed, you must be tired out."
"Oh, no, Mis' Richards. I'm used t' sech things.
I guess it's as well the Doc had me take him up.
I don't believe he'd a-fetched it by hisself."

A Useless Vacation

People who knew Martha after she was thirty
Recognized the appropriateness of her name.
She was "cumbered with much serving."
It was during her mother's long sickness
That Martha had gradually assumed command.
By the time her mother was up and around
She found Martha not only ran the house
But she also had her two brothers in charge,
To say nothing of the old hired man.
Somehow Martha's mother felt rather relieved to have
    burdens
Lifted from her shoulders even if it wasn't always
    pleasant.
It was a little like having Martha's father back.
He'd been the one to see to every little thing.
The boys were naturally easygoing like their mother.
They took Martha's busy ways tolerantly.
They frequently joked with their mother about it
And sometimes teased Martha herself.
As Martha grew older she seemed more and more
    "cumbered."
Everything had to be just so, and on her rested the
    burden
Of seeing that it was.
Not daring to leave the farm to anyone else's supervision
She never felt she ought to go away.

Finally, one fall, when she'd got as near caught up
As she ever expected to be this side of the grave,

She did agree to go with her mother for a three days'
      visit
With a favorite cousin who lived over the mountain.
Needless to say, Martha was busy "helping" those three
      days;
And had plenty of criticism to give her mother on her
      way back.
Arriving home, she was looking things over
Before she had even taken her bonnet off.
She went to the bay window in the sitting room.
"My lands!" she called out, "I never see the beat.
The way those men folks have let things go!
Here's Ma's best fuchsia all covered with red lice.
We might better stayed to home!"

An Impossible Place

Folks noticed along in the fall
That Mort didn't seem very spry.
He hadn't really ever been himself
Since he'd had that attack of grippe in the spring.
As cold weather came on, folks worried about him
Living there alone with meals to get and fires to tend.
Some of the neighbors got to bringing in hot dishes.
He always seemed to be pleased but he didn't get any
  better.
Finally, someone persuaded him to send for Henry.
Henry was his favorite nephew.
He lived down in the borough and wasn't working that
  winter
Except when he got some odd jobs of chopping.
Henry came up one Saturday afternoon.
That evening after they had finished the dishes,
Mort put in a big chunk and opened the front damper.
He asked about all the relatives down the valley.
Gradually he worked around to his own condition.
He told Henry what he'd never admitted before—
That he felt "awful peaked" and didn't have any
  strength.
He even admitted he hated the thought
Of being alone in the house all winter.
He went to the sink and pumped some water into the
  dipper,
And refilled the teakettle boiling on the stove.
Settling down again in his rocking chair,

He told Henry how he'd left him half of his estate in
his will.

"You and Willie'll git all of that—

Share and share alike. That ain't more'n fair t' Willie

Bein' as he's nephew t' me same as you be."

Mort rocked for a minute, looking at the stove.

Then he looked at Henry intently, leaning forward in his
chair.

"I like you, Henry. Allus took to yu sence you was *that*
high.

I'm gittin' along and I ain't what I used t' be.

I was thinkin' mebbe you'd feel like stayin' here to the
Union

Through the winter anyhow, and say—well, till I git
done.

Probably that ain't fur off."

Henry started to protest.

Mort stopped him evidently fearing he might say no.

"I've got $10,000 in bonds under th' mattress in there,"

He pointed toward the bedroom.

"It's yourn as soon as yu say you'll stay.

Me and you'd git along fine, Henry. I know we would."

Henry shook his head.

"Nope, Uncle Mort, I jest couldn't do it.

I like yu an' all that, but gosh!

I couldn't stan' it livin' way up here to the Union.

Why, they ain't even got Blue Stag chewin' to th' store."

An Oasis

Of course, intoxicating beverages were not sold legally
Anywhere in the state in those days.
In spite of this, thirsty ones were always able
To find unlawful oases in the legal Sahara.
Strangers in town soon found out
Who could tell them what doors to enter
If they were suffering from a thirst.
When there were especial celebrations in towns
People were employed to give such assistance.

One year there was such a celebration
Marking the anniversary of the Battle of Bennington.
Word had gone out that all the places selling liquor
Must be closed.

Aunt Mary was walking down the street
With a nephew and a niece in tow;
She had brought them down to the celebration.
Aunt Mary hated the demon rum with bitter hate,
And she never hesitated to express her feelings regarding
    it.
This day she passed a place which she, and many others,
Knew was supposed to be a saloon;
She stopped her two wards in front of it.
Looking at it with a rare disdain, she told them
Of the wickedness of the liquor traffic.
"Thank heaven," she said as they started on,
"There's *one* day they have to keep shut!"
A small boy had seen Aunt Mary stop

And look at the closed building.
As she started on he walked over to her.
"Yu can git in 'round back, Miss," he said,
Proud to be of service.

Intelligence

Mrs. Urban was boarding at the Park place.
A change in her financial condition
Had compelled her to stay in more humble quarters
Than she had been accustomed to.
Having been forced into the real country,
She set about "going in for it"
In her usual thorough manner.
She had only been on the farm a few days
When Charlie Park encountered her
Standing at the pasture bars.
She was gazing at the hills
At the foot of which the cows were grazing.
She hailed Charlie as a deliverer,
And begged him to escort her through the herd
So that she might reach the hills beyond.
Assuring her that the cattle were harmless,
Charlie led the way across the pasture.
Seeing a friend, the cows looked up, and drew near.
Mrs. Urban clutched Charlie's arm.
"They won't touch yu," Charlie reassured her.
"But they keep staring at me," she said, still gripping
    him fast.
Charlie yelled at the cattle,
And made a rush toward one, thus escaping Mrs. Urban's
    hold.
"They're jest curious," he said, over his shoulder.
Arriving at the other side of the pasture,
Mrs. Urban, relieved, stopped to look at the cows.

"They certainly have curiosity," she agreed,
"And they are *so* intelligent."

Park was speaking of the matter at the store, later.
"Then she says, 'They're *so* intelligent.'"
He picked up his bag of groceries.
"Good Lord! If they'd had a mite of intelligence
They wouldn't never 'a' looked at 'er twice."

A Real Hitching Post

Hen had often explained to folks he didn't know
How he had captured the cannon that guarded the green.
He gave the impression that he had annexed it at once
And kept it with him to bring home
When he came back from the war.
The afternoon a horse hitched in front of the store,
Startled by a small boy, jumped back and ran away,
Reminded Hen of something he'd forgotten for years.
It was the horse leaving the bridle behind,
With the rein securely tied to the post,
That brought it to mind.
Hen had sat for some moments in meditation.
Then he raised his head and took off his hat.
"We was close to the Rebs' lines," he said,
"And on that account I was guardin' th' Gen'l's tent."
Try as he might the name had slipped him.
"Up comes another gen'l with his horse in a lather.
'Hen,' he says— Seemed t' know me. Most of 'em did—"
He spat modestly to the left.
" 'Hen,' he says, 'hold my horse.' "
Hen shifted to the other cheek and went on.
"It wan't more'n five minutes afore the Rebs dropped a
    shell
And first I know that horse was blowed all to hell."
He stopped to let that sink in.
"The Gen'l come runnin' out th' tent.
'Where's m' horse?' he says, lookin' up and down.
I says, 'Gen'l, I don't know where in hell yer horse's
    gone,
But here's the bridle,' I says, handin' it to 'im."

The Card Players

Of course, there were many in the village
Who looked on card playing as a sin.
Those who saw no harm in a game of cribbage
Usually respected the feelings of others
And pulled the shades down when a game was on.
In several families there was a division of opinion;
The men folks saw no harm in it,
But their wives were very much set against it;
They felt the futures of their children
Might be endangered if they ever looked on cards.

That's why Lawyer Hicks
And George Bellows, the liveryman,
Used to play with Ed Brayley, the storekeeper,
In the back room of the store after closing time.
They met regularly Saturday nights.
At first they made excuses when they got home;
Then it got to be such a usual thing
That it was accepted by the wives, under protest.
The protests were not infrequent.

One Saturday night the party broke up
Just after midnight.
The players agreed to report on Monday
Exactly what each wife said when they got home.

"Well, Ed," Lawyer Hicks said, on Monday morning,
When he came into the store for his mail,
"What did your wife say Sat'day night?"

Ed smiled as he lighted his pipe.

"She give me the devil."

"Well, sir," Hicks reported,

"My wife just looked at me, and she says:

'Why, Henry!' and she might jest as well

Have given me what you got, and more."

George Bellows sat by the stove and chewed.

"What about you?"—they both turned to George.

George chuckled.

"My woman never said a word t' me," he said.

After a moment's pause, he added,

"She ain't sence, neither."

Consolation

For more than twenty years
Abbie Henderson and Julia Sands
Had lived together in the small cottage
Opposite the store in the village.
Abbie was small and wiry;
Julia was short and inclined to be fat.
Their dispositions were what would be expected
Of women of their physical characteristics.
In spite of the fact that they often disagreed,
They generally got along very comfortably.
When Abbie got too much "nerved up,"
Julia was a calming influence;
Julia's tendency to let things go
Was often corrected by Abbie's up-and-doing temper.
They each had a small income left by relatives,
And that, with their garden and chickens,
Gave them all they required for comfortable living.

As they grew older, people often wondered
How one would ever get along without the other.
Abbie had always seemed rather frail,
In spite of her continuous activity,
So when it was Julia who was stricken
Everybody was surprised.

The village had settled down to its routine
The day after Julia's funeral.
The minister's wife dropped in during the afternoon,
Thinking that Abbie must be prostrated.

She found her bustling about as usual.
They sat down in the sitting room—
Miss Abbie with some mending in her lap.
The minister's wife expressed her sympathy again
And told Abbie how hard these first days must be;
Then she went on to express her high regard
For Julia, and said how much she would be missed by all.
Finally, Abbie got up to light the lamp.
"Well," she said, as she turned the wick,
"I'll hev a lot more closet room than I did."

Jenny and Granny

When Jenny came to live with her grandmother
Some of the neighbors felt sorry for the small girl;
They knew that Grandfather Dill found life happier
Living up north with a son.
But Jenny seemed to be able to handle "Granny."
Arm in arm they walked up the street to the church,
And in the hymns Jenny's young voice
Covered the rough edges of Granny's tattered tones.
When Ike Schuyler put Granny's cow in pound
And tried to collect a dollar from her,
It was Jenny who calmly opened the gate and let the cow
    out.
She told Ike he should not impose on Granny any more;
He knew the cow was just on her way home.
Then, having expressed her mind, Jenny took three hops
And landing on the cow's back rode away in defiant
    triumph.
Jenny also made friends with Darwin Cook's crooked-
    legged horse.
Up to then only Darwin had dared to go near him.
Probably it was the same taming instinct
That worked on Granny and Darwin's horse.

One day Granny sent Jenny to the Point on an errand.
Jenny often went the three miles there and back at a trot
And this time Granny was in an especial hurry.
Part way there Jenny overtook a neighbor
Who stopped his fat, ambling horse
And insisted that Jenny should ride.

The small girl didn't know how to refuse,
But as the fat horse shuffled along through the dust
She grew more and more impatient.
Finally, she said in her most polite manner:
"If you don't mind, Mr. Boynton,
I think I'll get out and walk.
You see Granny's in a hurry for her things."
"And as I was crossin' th' bridge into the Point,"
Mr. Boynton told Granny afterwards,
"Wan't that little tyke a-trottin' out
With her errants tucked under her arm."

A Sure Sign

"Yes, we got through the winter pretty tol'able.
One er two th' old folks dropped out;
They allus do come spring.
They manage to hang on through th' winter;
Then, jest when it seems though life was wuth livin',
Like enough they jest peter out.
How? No, I ain't never figgered it out 'cept—
Well, sometimes I've thought they go along
Whilst everythin' was restin' under th' snow;
When there wan't much bein' done 'cept th' chores;
When they set a good deal 'round the fire.
That jest suits th' old folks.
But with the stirrin' round that spring brings,
The old folks ain't got anythin' in 'em t' git stirred up.
There ain't no sap to rise, as yu might say,
And they jest git left futher an' futher behind—
Then all t' once they quit.
That's how I figger it.

"Old man Pease?
Well, I wan't sure but he'd peter out come spring.
He was kinda peaked all winter,
And some th' neighbors was sure it 'ud be 'Widder Pease'
    'fore long.
We got so we kinda watched th' old man—
Waitin' t' see how he'd act, come th' first warm day.

"Well, sir, it come 'bout three weeks ago.
It started out mild as yu please, purty soon arter sun-up.

By cracky! I sez, if Old Man Pease don't feel nothin'
   t'day
He's as good as buried.
So I was real tickled when 'long 'bout noon I looked out
An' there was Pease hobblin' past with his wife's shawl
Wrapped 'round his old shoulders.
He was headed straight fer th' store.

"You can allus tell that way.
If on a day like that un
A feller don't git down t' the store and set,
There ain't much hope fer 'im."

Foundations

By the time Jake Harmon was in his teens
He had the physique of a grown man.
Because he was always knocking into things,
He was generally known as "Bumble."
His awkwardness, and especially the size of his feet,
Were always furnishing amusement for the village.
He suffered from frequent misjudgment
From people who expected his mind to be as grown up
   as his body.
As a rule he was good-natured, but at times
He used his strength to punish fun that had gone too far.
When he came to man's estate he took his place
Among the solid citizens of the village.

Oscar Dow had gone West at the time
Jake was the village joke; and when
He came back some years later for a visit
His attitude toward all those who had stayed at home
Was one of unpleasant condescension.
He was telling a group in front of the store
About the superior virtues of life in the great West,
When Jake drove up in his sagging buckboard
And, getting out, started toward the store.
Oscar went over to meet him.
He had the same expression he would have had for Jake
At the time he had left the village.
"Well, well, here's the village big boy, bigger than ever."
Jake's not too cordial handshake was nevertheless painful.
"Save the bones, old man," Oscar said.

"I never could understand the need of so much waste in you, Jake.

Look at the underpinning!" he exclaimed, turning toward the group.

Jake put his hands into his pockets and stared at Oscar's feet.

Then he said, slowly:

"Well, Oscar, they wouldn't put the same foundation under a henhouse

That they would under a church, even out West, would they?"

The String Bean Business

The sign, made of a weathered board,
Was nailed to a not-too-upright fence post
Which helped to support two strands
Of sagging barbed wire.
The wire enclosed, in a manner of speaking,
The dooryard of the Bump place;
The sign read PEAS FOR SALE—
Both "s's" were facing the wrong way.

Mrs. Sims, who had bought a place across the valley,
Stopped her shining roadster and honked her horn.
Sam Bump appeared from the back of the house
And shoved his straw hat from his forehead
(Which was as far as he would go in the matter of defer-
    ence).
He "guessed" he could let Mrs. Sims have a mess of peas.

By the time Mrs. Sims was ready to depart with the peas
Sam had acquainted her with considerable local history,
As he stood with one foot on the running board.
She had stepped on the starter when Sam turned to her
    again.
"You folks like string beans?" he asked.
Mrs. Sims assured him they were very fond of them.
"Well then," Sam said, waving an arm toward the
    garden,
"You jest come up an' help yerselves;
We ain't raisin' no hogs this year."

To Get to the Cove

Nate Barrows leaned on the fence
With one foot on the second board.
His unshaven chin rested on the top rail.
His eyes followed the growing load of hay
The "Walker Boys" were putting on
With their new-fangled hay loader.
Nate viewed the labor-saving contraption with scorn.
Although few could corroborate his testimony,
He liked to tell of his prowess with the hay fork.
The size of the tumbles he could lift to a load,
And the speed with which he worked
Were things no longer to be seen.
One of the small boys was raking after,
Proud of his ability with the horse
And in imminent danger of falling from the rake.
Nate heard a car coming and straightened up.
It slowed down and stopped near him.
A woman disguised with dark glasses
Spoke from the driver's seat.
"Are you acquainted hereabouts?" she asked.
Nate unfastened himself from the supporting fence.
His affronted dignity needed no artificial prop.
By the time Nate had proved his nativeness
The tourist was getting anxious to go on.
She finally managed to ask him
How to get to Turner's Cove.
"Oh, you're goin' to the Cove, be yu?"
There was more talk to show he knew the Cove.
The tourist reminded Nate that what she most wanted

Was to know how to get there.
Nate pointed down the road.
"You jest keep goin' down the rud 'bout two miles.
They's a new concrete bridge there."
He paused and she nodded.
"Wal, t' git t' th' Cove you turn off
'Bout half a mile this side that bridge."

The New Rug

When Etta married Oscar Hoyt
Everybody knew that Oscar's easygoing ways
Were at an end.
Even at the wedding Etta never fully lost
The determined set of her mouth.
She seemed to want to have the formalities over
So she could get right down to something practical.
It was all she could do to keep from taking a hand
When the refreshments were being served.
She had insisted on doing some of the cooking,
And what she made, she made of the best there was.
Quality was part of her creed of thrift.
She would work her fingers to the bone to get, or to save,
But when she did buy anything she had to have the best.
Buying a new winter coat was a matter of weeks of deliberation.
When she got it she had paid three times as much
As most of her neighbors would have done.
She was wearing hers, however, when they were buying again.
There was not a cheap or shoddy thing in her house.
Everything about her was good quality—
Everything except her life,
Wholly taken up with saving money and getting things.
She had planned for two years
On buying a new rug for the parlor.
Not that the rag carpet there had much wear
But it just wasn't good enough.
She scanned the catalogs and compared prices.

Every time she was near a large store she looked.
Finally, she bought a little hurriedly
Because she was going to entertain the Sewing Society.
The first evening the new rug—light-colored in the center
With a dark border, quite deep—
Was on the floor
The Minister came to call.
Oscar, being a little hard of hearing,
Drew his rocker over toward the Minister.
Etta was distressed when he dragged the chair on the new
    rug.
When he planted his feet on the light-colored part
Her lips tightened.
She cleared her throat several times
And coughed discreetly into her handkerchief.
The Minister asked if she had a cold.
Oscar paid no attention.
Finally, he stretched his long legs out.
The sharp heel of his heavy shoe
Pressed into the soft nap of the new rug.
Etta couldn't stand it any longer.
"Excuse me interrupting, Reverend,"
She said, sitting forward on her straight-backed chair,
"But it does seem t' me, Oscar,
You could manage t' sit with your feet on the dark
    border."

The Borough Goes Dry

Of course, there was always some excitement
Over Town Meeting in the Borough.
It usually centered in the fight for selectman,
Or over who should be road commissioner.
Miss Willing had been town clerk so long
That nobody else was ever thought of for that job.
When local option came up the wets got busy
And the town voted to allow beer to be sold.
Ed Pelley enlarged his filling station
And put in a lunchroom so he could get a license.
Business was quite brisk that year
What with the local trade and thirsty tourists.
Ed's wife was a good cook and her pies got a reputation.
The next year Ed built an addition;
He covered the rough timber with matched boards
And finished it all natural.
Mrs. Ed put curtains up at the windows
And Ed installed a cash register.
Some of the local customers thought it was too fancy
But their thirsts overcame their dislike.
Then the lumber job shut down
And the Borough began to feel the depression.
When next Town Meeting came around,
There were a number of citizens
Who couldn't pay their taxes and so lost their votes.
When the ballots were counted it was found
That the drys had won by nine votes.
It was a sad group that met at Ed's place that night.
"It ain't right," he said as he put the glasses on the table.

"I ben goin' over the list;
There was a dozen o' my best customers—
'Nuff t' carried fer license—
Deprived o' their votin' rights
Jest because they had hard luck and couldn't pay their
   taxes.
'Tain't right."

Chivalry

The Haswell place had once been a good farm.
It began to go down when the sheep business
Had been given over to the West.
The last Haswell to try to run it
Had finally given up and moved to the village.
He rented the place for some years
And then he sold it for what it would bring.
Grover Strong had never paid off the mortgage
And gradually the interest piled up.
That was the only thing that grew there,
Except a little hay in the south meadow.
The rest was going back to forest.

Grover was sitting on the sagging porch
When a city visitor came up the hill.
He greeted Grover and sat down on the step.
He spoke of the view across the valley,
Of the peace of the surrounding woods.
"I suppose it gets pretty well buried in winter,"
He said, feeling he had been showing too much feeling.
Grover allowed it did bank up with snow some.
"I recollect last winter," he said, leaning forward.
"We hed one old heller of a snow storm.
The woman went down t' th' foot th' hill there
T' fetch a couple o' pails o' water from th' spring.
I stood here in th' doorway watchin' 'er.
A gust o' wind 'd come and I couldn't see 'er.
Then it'd quiet down and there she'd be, a-wallerin'."
He sank back in his chair.
"B' gol! They was times I wan't sure she'd make it."

Mail Time

Two horses were hitched to the much-chewed posts
In front of Brayley's general store.
One stood with his head down paying little attention
To the flies, except for a languid swishing of its tail.
The end of one rein with which it was tied
Lay partly buried in the dust under the mare's front foot.
The other occupant of the hitching area
Stamped first one foot and then the other.
Its tail swished continuously and its head tossed.
It was anchored with a stout leather halter
Which was buckled on over the headstall.

Inside, the leisurely Brayley was sorting the mail.
Ike Loveland sat on a nail keg with his head bowed,
Paying as little attention to things
As his mare outside.
Jim Lovett walked nervously from one thing to another.
It was easy to tell which man owned which horse.
You might wonder how soon the horses would have
    changed
If the owners had swapped.

Finally, Brayley stood in front of the small window
In the middle of the mail boxes and said: "That's all."
Ike Loveland glanced toward his box and saw it was
    empty.
He leaned back and stretched his legs and yawned.
"If I don't git no letters I don't hev t' write none," he
    said.

Jim Lovett hurried to the window and took the letters
That Brayley handed him.
He started to the door looking them over on the way.
He was going down the steps when he stopped and hur-
ried back.
Brayley had just settled down with the paper.
Jim stuck his head in at the window.
"Say, Brayley," he said in a demanding tone,
"Where in hell's my *Christian Herald?*"

Freedom Rings

A New York lawyer had bought the Evans place.
It had once been a fairly good farm,
But since the last of the Evans family had died
It had been rented, by the out-of-town relatives
To whom it had been left, to a shiftless family.
But now the new owner announced that he was giving up
   the law
And coming "back to the land."

He was discussing the matter one day at the store
Where Billy Pines, his next-door neighbor, had met him
And introduced him to some of his fellow townsmen.
Waxing eloquent about life on a farm, the lawyer told
   them
How it offered a man the only life of security and free-
   dom today.
He enlarged on the boss-ridden condition of the cities,
The domination of the labor unions,
And the financial insecurity due to taxes.
"You men don't realize how well off you are," he went
   on.
"You are independent, free. Nobody tells you
What hours you are to work, nor your hired men, either."
He walked up and down by the counter.
"You fellows just don't know how well off you are."

Billy Pines, feeling himself a little responsible,
Hitched himself back on the counter:
"Well, I guess mebbe you're right. We don't," he said.

"We kin work from four in th' mornin' t' nine at night—
And I guess most of us does. No labor boss t' prevent
  neither.
I reckon we're fairly independent, as you say.
If we git good plantin' weather in th' spring,
A good growin' summer—not too dry, nor not too wet—
And a good spell o' weather come harvest,
An' providin' some new bug or disease don't set in on us,
We're pretty sure o' gittin' a good lot o' crops.
Then if prices ain't too all-fired low—bein' good crops—
Like enough we'll git 'nuff cash in
T' pay the int'rest and taxes, and mebbe shingle th' shed."
He let his feet swing in a gesture of freedom:
"Nope. It's true. Nobody's bossin' us farmers."

Uncle Billy

Ever since he had passed the eighty-five mark
Uncle Billy had been a cross for the pious to bear.
He had always been a sinner.
Either that or else his moral code
Was not that of the village.
Worse than all that he was not penitent in his old age.
He seemed to be enjoying life to the full
Even though he was well on his way to the dark valley.
His chief regret seemed to be
That he was too old to get the pleasure out of things
That once gave him enjoyment.
He did cut his alcoholic rations somewhat,
But only because his income was somewhat cut.
He liked all kinds of people.
Often those who were considered outcasts
Found in Uncle Billy an understanding friend.
He used to sit on his front porch
With his cane hanging on the back of his chair.
If it was chilly his housekeeper, who was almost as old as
    he,
Would insist on putting a shawl around his shoulders.
As soon as she went inside, Uncle Billy would remove it.
"I don't want to appear effeminate," he'd say.

One afternoon he was sitting in his chair dosing
When a Salvation Army man came along.
He walked briskly up the steps and touched his cap.
"Have you fifty cents to give the Lord?" he asked.
Uncle Billy smiled at him with his blue eyes.

"How old are you, young man?"

"I'm twenty-seven."

Uncle Billy hitched himself up in his chair.

"I guess you'd better give me *your* fifty cents for the Lord.

I'll be seeing him sooner than you will."

Parsimony

People excused Etta Short's parsimony
On the ground that she had worked so hard
For what little she had.
It was true she had worked hard all her life
But necessary frugality
Had grown into downright miserliness.
She had even held back her affections
So that her children left home as soon as they could,
And left gladly.
She kept on working and saving until she wore out.
Even when she could stay up only part of the day
She wouldn't have any help.
She'd manage to get to the stove and light a fire
Under one griddle, as she always did,
To make herself some tea.
Finally, the daughter stepped in.
She hired a good woman to live with her mother
And she herself came to see her each day.
They said Etta softened up considerably before she died.

When she was in her prime
She told the butcher's boy, one Saturday,
To bring five cents' worth of liver for the cat.
She was having a piece of pork—
The only piece of meat she'd had that week.
When the boy brought her the meat a little later,
She was waiting by the front gate.
"D'je bring me th' liver fer m' cat?"

The boy handed her the small package.
"Well, you kin take it right back.
I don't want it.
The cat jest ketched a bird."

A Horse Trader

Because Stub Hankins was rarely seen
Doing any manual labor
He was looked on by the village as lazy and shiftless.
His place certainly showed no care
And Stub was decidedly neglectful of his appearance.
He was a horse trader by profession,
And in spite of his reputation for laziness
He made a comfortable living at it.
There were times when he was hard up
But most of the time he had plenty for his family,
And not infrequently he was well off.
He was absolutely reliable in his dealings
With anybody but a horse trader.
The village doctors always got their horses from Stub.
He knew what they wanted and saw that they had it.
But his real enjoyment was in trading just to trade.
He knew it was a battle of wits
And that no quarter would be given.
None of the intricacies of high finance
Were ever more devious than the ways of horse traders.

One afternoon Stub drove past the hotel.
He had a mare hitched to the buggy.
"F.H." was standing in front of the hotel
And he called out to Stub:
"Where'd you get that piece of horse-flesh?"
"Traded fer 'er," Stub said.
"How old is she?"

Stub stretched a leg over the dash.
"Wal, the feller said she was fifteen.
He's such a damned liar though,
Like enough she ain't more'n ten."

A Horse-Loving Parson

Usually the minister's horse
Had been the safe plodding style
To which no horseman in the borough
Would pay any attention, except to make fun of it.
When Parson Anderson drove into town,
His horse was the first thing that attracted attention.
Even the hardened sinners agreed that she was some
  stepper.
The deacons were a little worried about it.
It was all right to like "hoss flesh,"
But for a minister of the gospel to own a steed
With racing blood in her veins didn't seem quite safe.
He hadn't been there long when he made himself wel-
  come
At Rodney Shank's blacksmith shop.
Then some of the Ladies' Society felt something should
  be said.
No fault could be found with the parson's preaching.
He was sound and his delivery acceptable.
He seemed to carry out his parish duties properly.
All of the complaints boiled down to the influences
Which seemed to center in his bay mare.
They all stopped to look when the parson drove down
  the street
In his trim cutter, his mare's coat glistening
As she made the snow fly with her fast-moving feet.
Rodney Shanks wasn't the only one who tried to get the
  parson
To take her to the ice races on the lake in York State.

The parson only shook his head and said:
"Some of the folks wouldn't understand."
Rodney was shoeing the parson's mare one day
And they were alone in the shop.
The parson watched Rodney heat the iron and then shape
    it.
"I wish I could work on my material like that," he said.
Rodney pumped the bellows a minute slowly.
"Wal, parson, mebbe you'd get on with shapin' 'em up
    better
If you cud run 'em through the fire *fust*
Stead o' jest threatenin' 'em with it arterwards."

Why Eph Came Back

Ephraim Halleck had gone West
Along with most of the able-bodied people
From his section of the state.
Most of the emigrants were younger than Eph,
But he could hold up his end with any of them.
His fifty-odd years had whitened his hair,
But his adventuring spirit led a body
Which had the spring of youth in it.
So Ephraim went to Ohio
Where the corn grew higher than a man on horseback,
Out of soil reeking with fertility.
He went with his wondering wife
And his eager sons and daughters.

When Ephraim came back to Vermont
He was nearing seventy and he was still active.
His wife was buried in the Ohio soil
And his sons plowed the acres
Which were added to those their father had left.
Eph came back to Vermont full of stories
Of the wonders of the West.
He never tired of these tellings,
But his old friends, who hadn't prospered
By sticking to their rocky farms,
Got sick of hearing of the wealth come by so easily.
It was Ben Judson who finally gave voice
To what they'd all come to feel.
"Well, Eph," he snapped, "if that Ohio country
Is sech an awful good section t' live in,

Why in tunkit didn't yu stay there?"
Eph looked startled and then a little hurt.
He looked off at the hills before he spoke.
"Boys, I'll tell yu.
I couldn't be satisfied t' live all m' days
Where water don't run downhill."

Piety Hill

The Templetons were pious folks.
That's why they call the hill up yonder,
Past the church,
Where they and all their folks have lived for years,
"Piety Hill."
And they really thought they were better than the rest.
Didn't they always sit on the mourners' bench
Every winter when the whole town
Got its soul renewed
With tales full enough of fire and brimstone
To set the church itself on fire?
As I said, those Templetons were pious
And yet sometimes you'd hear how Jed,
The old man, would go to town some miles away
And sell a side of beef or else some pork
When all the neighbors knew
They didn't raise a critter on the place—
Or hardly one.
Other things they took, so 'twas said,
But no one thought to sift it out
And bring them up before the law.
They made a handy thing to blame
When cattle went astray, or a farm-tool
Left in the meadow overnight
Could not be found.
You couldn't prove they took a thing,
Not before a court at any rate.
And besides all that
We'd known their folks and they were neighbors.

Steve Benchley was boarded by the town.
For years each Town Report came out
With twelve items which read like this:
"Board and lodging for S. Benchley
One month . . . twelve dollars."
He had some trouble with his heart.
It wasn't strange his heart was ailing
When he hadn't kith or kin and scarce a friend.
Miss Ellis, who'd boarded him for years,
Passed on, and her man moved to the Falls.
Then the Selectmen sent Steve
To board on Piety Hill at the Templetons'.

He'd been there near a year when March came around
And the voters met to discuss taxes
And elect officers for the ensuing year.
This done there was a pause and Steve arose.
"Fellow cit'zens," he said in a quavering voice,
"The Good Book says there was a man
Going down to Jericho who fell among thieves.
I'm that man,
And I want you should change my boardin' place."

The Widow's Smite

In spite of the fact that the Widow Sloopstead
Had lived in town for a number of years,
Nobody seemed to know much about her history.
It was generally understood, however, that she had one.
This conclusion was arrived at to some extent
By her reputation after she arrived in town.
The horses of various residents had been observed
Hitched to a tree in her backyard.
Finally, Billy Otter came to be her one steady admirer.
Billy lived alone on a small farm not far from the
  widow's house.
He ran a peddler's cart when he wasn't working on his
  farm.
His high wagon was a familiar sight on the roads
For several miles around.
On his way home he always stopped at the widow's.
Observing neighbors noticed he usually carried a pail
When he came out to get into his cart again.

One spring the Widow Sloopstead went away on the train.
When she came back a few weeks later
She was accompanied by an elderly man.
She announced to the station agent that she was now Mrs.
  Brown.
The next day, after her arrival with her new husband,
She went out and stopped Billy Otter as he was passing.
A friend who was riding with Billy reported later
That the widow had told Billy that she was married.
"I've married a real nice man," she said.

"I'm agoin' t' settle down and be respectable.
And, Billy Otter, I want you should take your garbage
  pail
Off my back porch for good and all."

Nothing to Crow About

After looking like no-man's land
For several weeks of showers and sunshine
The road in front of the Burr sisters
Had at last dried out.
For a long time the wagons that had wallowed through
Would have that mud caked on the wheels.
The wind for the first time in months
Brought no chill with it.
The Burr sisters' piazza was draped with bedding.
Blankets hung from the line put up for winter washings
And feather beds bulged from upstairs windows.
The two sisters darted in and out
Always carrying something.
They never stopped to hear the robins or the bluebirds
Nor to sense the something brought on the south wind
Which is the essence of spring.
There were things that must be done
Perhaps to deaden something which might be felt.
Addie, the younger one, did stop when she was alone,
And look off across the fields and away beyond for a
    minute,
While the south wind blew her hair across her face.
Just then her sister came out on the piazza,
A roll of rag rugs under her arm.
The rooster, making valuable discoveries for his flock in
    the road,
Flapped his wings and crowed his gladdest.
Miss Burr picked up the stick she used to beat the rugs

And rushed out toward the busy brood.
"Go on back off this road," she called.
"You darned old fool, you, standin' there crowin'
With eggs only fetchin' twenty-five cents a dozen."

A New Feeling

The steps before the front door slanted
And the bottom tread was broken.
The thawing ground was covered with chips
Mixed with pale potato parings, eggshells, and bones.
All around, within easy throwing distance,
These relics were coated with fuzzy grease
From the winter offerings of dishwater.
The door, partly open, showed a box cover patch
Where one panel had been broken in.
Zed was sitting on a chopping block
Throwing scraps of pork rind to four hounds
Whose evident bone structure explained their greed.
Zed's winter crop of graying hair
Stuck out over his ears from the pressure of his hat.
His pipe slanted from his mouth to the spot
Where his necktie would have been if he'd ever worn one.
A thin wisp of smoke drifted from the rusty stovepipe
Which answered for a chimney.
A neighbor was leaning against the hitching post.
Zed had lost his "woman" a week before,
And the neighbor had come up, at his wife's suggestion,
To see how Zed was getting along.
Zed had been telling how lonesome he felt
And how he couldn't settle down
To the little work he had to do.
He sat looking at the ground.
Without looking up he said:
"I've lost a lot o' dawgs—good uns too—
But I ain't never felt like this—*not never.*"

A Pleasant Rumor

Miss Primer was not a typical old maid.
She was plump and red-cheeked
And she had a nice smile.
She lived alone, to be sure,
But she did not keep a cat nor a canary.
She did have a dog but it was not of the lap variety.
It was a friendly Irish Setter.

Then she had not been without beaus.
She had been popular in her younger days
But somehow men seemed to tire of her.
The impression was that she was too smiling.
Not that she had any real sense of humor.
She really didn't have much of any sense,
And after being in her company for a short time
Her men friends found her quite sickish.
Sometimes they spoke of her as "that sugar bowl."
The time her father was in his last sickness
People would meet her on the street
And ask how he was.
With the usual smile and bubbling manner,
She'd say: "He's worse, thank you."

One day the postmaster handed her the mail.
Looking over his glasses he told her
He'd heard a rumor around town
That she was married.
He hadn't seen her for a few days
And he began to think it must be true.

She smiled and dimpled as usual.

"Oh, no, Mr. Potter, there ain't a word of truth in it."

She looked down at the paper in her hand.

"But thanks for the rumor, Mr. Potter."

The Parasol

Tuesday was going to be a red-letter day,
For Edie's father had sent the postcard
To the uncle who lived in Danby.
Of course, Edie was too small to read it,
But it said:
"We are sending parcel up on morning train.
Do not fail to be at station to get it."
By Monday night the family was worn out
With answering Edie's questions
And persuading her that she did not need a trunk
When she was going to spend the day.
Tuesday morning she could hardly eat her breakfast.
She had her favorite doll in one hand
And in the other held her joy and pride—
It was a small ruffled parasol.
It was made of silk with pink rosebuds on it.
Edie's good-by kisses were perfunctory.
She trudged down the hill with her father,
Chattering like a magpie.
She urged him to hurry.
She might miss the train.
At the station she was determined
To get out on the track to see if the train was coming.
When it did come, hissing and blowing,
She got as close to her father as possible.
But when her father introduced her to the conductor,
Whose blue suit had lots of shining buttons on it,
She forgot all about being scared.
He took her by the hand and lifted her up the steps

Just as the train started.
Perhaps she kissed her father good-by.
She was too excited to know.
It was just as they were going into the car
That the kindly conductor tried to take her parasol,
Suggesting that she would want it closed in the train.
Edie grasped the smooth handle firmly.
The idea of hiding from the passengers' view
Those beautiful rosebuds was not to be thought of.
So with her parasol held aloft she walked down the aisle
Escorted by the smiling conductor.
And all the way to Danby she sat on the edge of the seat
With the parasol over her.

And now, a grandmother, no matter where she must
    travel,
She still refuses to put her bright parasol down.

Molly Miller

Except for the crusted drifts in the hollows
And on the north sides of the houses
The snow of winter had left the valley.
The warm sun was sending the deeper snows on the
  mountain
Rushing down each ravine
In a mad race to the overflowing river.
The listening ear could hear the urgence of spring
Surging in the soaked earth.
From the hills came the cawing of crows in flight.
Robins and bluebirds had been reported
To the sitters in the village store.

Molly Miller walked toward the village from the farm.
She walked with her head thrown back
And her step had the buoyancy of spring.
She looked at the hills and the valley
Searching for each sign of new life.
She breathed in the heady pungence of the damp fields.

As she came to the village street,
She met Mrs. Benton coming from the store
With Miss Draper who lived alone on the edge of the
  village.
Molly smiled and greeted them as she passed.
Their conversation stopped.
They both turned to look at Molly again.
Mrs. Benton was the first to speak.
"Why, what's happened to Molly Miller?

Why—she's beautiful!"
Miss Draper grudgingly admitted
That she might become so someday.
"But she's beautiful now," Mrs. Benton persisted.
"That smile just bowled me over."
Miss Draper shrugged her thin shoulders.
"Well, she has got a nice set o' teeth."
She paused, feeling she'd gone too far.
"But it does seem's though she shows 'em
Further back than they's any need to."

An Agreeable Man

There was one thing about Sol
That folks could always be sure of:
He'd never disagree with them in words.
He might sometimes show his disapproval
By retiring into complete silence,
But he'd never argue about anything.
He was able to maintain his position of peace
By never expressing an opinion
Until he was sure how the other person felt.
He would flounder around on the rim,
Using as much intelligence as he would have needed
To form an opinion of his own,
In an endeavor to find out how the other fellow stood.
Having found out, he might be quite strong
In his expressions of coinciding belief.
Sol chewed tobacco.
He made a dainty job of it, however.
His quid was always unobtrusive .
And his jaw worked the short and rapid stroke style.
Having attended to his chewing,
He would put that aside and do his talking.
This alternation gave him time to arrange his words
To suit his hearer's opinion.
If he had nothing to say the chewing
Might last for several measures.
One summer, after haying,
Sol was sitting on the store steps.
A drummer came out of the store and lit a cigar.
He passed the time of day with Sol.

"Well, what do folks up here think of our governor?"

Sol chewed for several bars in quick time.

"The gov'nor? I ain't heered nobody say nothin' agin 'im."

He chewed for a moment and then shifted his leg.

"Then again I ain't heered nothin' said fer 'im."

George Stone Loses Confidence

George Stone was sitting in the bar
At the station.
He was slowly drinking a glass of beer.
The old surrey, he drove as a stage to the village,
With old Kate hitched to it,
Was in its usual place outside.
Old Kate, with her head bowed,
Stamped, and switched flies, in the hot sun.
Suddenly something stung her.
In a moment she was just a cloud of dust
Disappearing up the road.
As she started, a boy rushed into the bar
And yelled at George.
"Oh, nobe," he replied, sipping his beer,
"Old Kade won'd run."
(George always seemed to have a bad cold.)
"Wal, she's runnin' now!" the boy shouted.
"Nobe. Guess you're mistagen.
Old Kade won'd run."
In desperation the boy screamed:
"But she will, too! She's half way to the village now."

George put down his beer and walked slowly to the door.
He saw no Kate in the accustomed place.
Away up the road there was a small cloud of dust.
Very deliberately he returned to his beer.
He took a swallow and put the glass down;
He shook his head and sighed.
"Well, boys,
I've lost all gonfidence id old Kade."

The Widow

A raw November wind
Was blowing the smoke from Widow Ellis' chimney
Flat along the ridge of her small house.
In her woodshed attic
Bunches of catnip hung from the rafters;
Below, in the shed, the wood was neatly piled—
Split wood on the north side,
Chunks and kindling on the south.
For twenty-odd years she had been "Widow Ellis."
She lived in the small house part way up Cemetery Hill,
Her only companions two black cats.
Her small pension was augmented
By the sale of eggs,
From a flock of hens which always laid.
She made rugs, too, from the rags the neighbors gave her,
And as the "Summer Folks" increased
She found a ready sale for them.
In the summer you'd see her
Busy in her garden, her face hidden by a faded sun-
    bonnet.
Now that it was cold she wore a black shawl
Pinned tight around her head,
And her husband's old blue army coat
Buttoned only at the top button.
One of the city folks dropped in to say good-by
And to order some more rugs.
As she was leaving she spoke of the long winter.
"What do you do to keep yourself busy, Mrs. Ellis,
During the long winter days?"

Mrs. Ellis, standing in the doorway
With her arms rolled up in her apron, sniffed.
"My lands, if you'd ever had two wood-stoves t' feed
You wouldn't be askin' any such fool question.
Keep busy? My lands!"

Free Wheeling

Jim Thayer was a good judge of horse flesh.
Being in the livery business he had to be.
He was a philosopher, too,
And used his knowledge of "hosses"
To help him judge human traits.
He used to say, speaking of humans,
That he "nevah really knew a fust class trottah
To be wuth much as a drivin' hoss."

One day George Spalding came into the stable office
Where Jim sat in front of a wood-stove,
With blankets and robes hung about the room,
And the rack of whips near the door.
George wanted to get a rig for the day,
But, as usual, he had no money.
"I'll pay yu, Jim, jest as soon as I git it,
But I got to take the woman over into York State.
You see her pa died."
Jim knew the family George had married into.
"I tell yu, George,
You can have the best rig I got in the place,
And the pick o' my hosses for nothin',
Any time you want t' bury one o' them Kittridges."

The Five Hundred

All winter Will Crawford, who drove the stage,
Had carried the women to the weekly meetings
Of the Five Hundred Club—
Pleasant gatherings at the various houses
Where a few hours of playing Five Hundred
Were followed by an hour's gossip
Over hot rolls, salad, and a cup of coffee.
In summer the club did not meet.

The Summer Colonists had all arrived
And Mrs. Willis gave a tea for them,
And invited a group of "Natives," too.
Will Crawford was called on
To take the party of "Natives"
Out to the imposing estate of Mrs. Willis.
Returning, after the tea, Miss Ellen Berry,
One of the faithful members of the Five Hundred Club,
Handed Will Crawford fifty cents.
He cleared his throat, as he always did—
He made so many dry remarks—
"It'll be a dollar," he said.
"My lands, Will Crawford, a dollar?
You always carry us, and fetch us,
To the Five Hundred for fifty cents."
Will cleared his throat again.
"That's all right for the Five Hundred,
But when you go buttin' into the Four Hundred
It'll cost y' a dollar."

Grandma Burton's Children

Mrs. Burton's children were all grown
But she still had the mothering habit.
To all the village children
She was always "Grandma Burton."
She had a parlor full of wonders—
A jug covered with things
From the four corners of the earth,
All pressed into putty;
A what-not in the corner containing such treasures
That no afternoon was long enough
To fully disclose its delights.
Best of all there was a stone crock
Under the shelf in her pantry
Which was always full of caraway cookies.

A little girl from the city
Got the habit of stopping with her nurse,
And augmenting her late breakfast—
As well as curtailing her lunch—
With a mid-morning feast of Grandma Burton's cook-
  ies.
Noticing a lack of interest in her luncheon,
The little girl's mother forbade the cookies.
The next day she walked into the enchanted parlor,
And after a tour of the chief wonders, she sniffed.
"Gammer Burton, seems to me I smell cookies."
This was too much for the old lady's soft heart,
And she brought forth half a cookie on a plate.

Her small guest looked at it a minute.
Heaving a small sigh, she said,
"You wouldn't think I could smell such a small piece,
Would you, Gammer Burton?"

Charlie Gets Out of Step

It was back in the Harrison and Morton campaign.
They had a big rally at Bennington,
And every band and drum corps for miles around
Paraded there,
Their brilliant uniforms glittering
In the hot August sun.
After three solid hours of marching
In the heat and dust, they didn't feel so brave
As their uniforms made them appear.
The Drum Corps from our town
Made quite a hit with their snappy rendering
Of the popular campaign airs.
Charlie Williams carried the bass drum.
He had so much of himself in front
That he appeared to carry two drums.
He had refreshed himself frequently,
And as they proceeded along a picket fence
He found it handy to lean against.
He was sliding his elbow along it
When he came to an open gate.
Suddenly missing his support
He and the drum entered the gate precipitately,
Landing in a heap at the foot of three steps.
Frank Bowen, the fifer, ceased playing;
He leaned over the fence and drawled,
"Charlie, ain't yu a leetle mite out o' step?"

A Roving Disposition

The family wasn't much.
They belonged to the lower stratum—
A mixture of sediments.
She had a sort of wild beauty
Which had proved attractive to various men
Before she settled down with Len.
They had a daughter Lizzie, now past twenty,
Who was fast following in her mother's steps.
One fall day Len came into the blacksmith's shop
And draped his lanky frame over a chair,
A picture of woe.
Wiping his faded eyes with an old bandanna,
He drawled, almost crying,
"Lizzie's went and runned off."
He got his audience at once.
"Her 'n' that Frenchman lit out last night
And I won't never see my Liz again."
He buried his face in his hands.
Remembering at least two other elopements
In Lizzie's young life,
His friends assured him she'd return before winter.
"Nope. I won't never see her again," he wailed.
Old man Allen left his forge,
And drank from the rusty dipper in the water pail.
"Now, Len," he said, "quit yer blattin'.
I tell yu she'll be back a-fore snow flies.
She takes after her ma.
She allus had that same rovin' disposition."

Always Hollerin'

When the neighbors heard Charlie Barney
Whistling about his place,
And saw him playing with his black spaniel,
They used to say:
"Hello! Guess Charlie's having a vacation."
They meant that Mrs. B. had gone over the mountain
To visit her sister.
The only affection in that household
Existed between Charlie and his dog.
Between Charlie and his wife there was an armed truce,
Not infrequently broken.

One Monday morning they were doing the washing.
Charlie had brought in the tubs,
Filled the boiler on the stove,
And built a good hot fire.
He was slowly turning the wringer,
His thoughts outside the window,
Where the hens were having a party in "her posey bed."
Suddenly the wringer turned hard
And he put on more steam.
A wild yell demanded his attention.
He had turned Mrs. B.'s arm into the wringer
Half way up to the elbow.

A few days later, he was getting some groceries,
When someone asked him about the accident.
He told the story briefly, without feeling.

"But didn't your wife make an outcry?"
He picked up his packages, and turned toward the door,
"Oh, yes. She hollered.
But, Lord!—she's always hollerin'."

Buying a Judge

Barker was a fair lawyer,
And probably if he hadn't been so lazy
He would have been a successful one.
He took cases others wouldn't touch,
And usually lost them.
He expended the wits he should have used
To win cases,
In explaining to his clients
Why he'd lost.
When he failed to get Cy Stiles off
In his trial for stealing pork
From his neighbor's cellar,
He carried his excuses a little too far.
"You cud buy that Judge fer a shillin',"
He had said, and the Judge had overheard.
Barker was called before the Court
On a charge of contempt.
He pleaded guilty—there was nothing else to do—
And was let off, providing he'd apologize.
He made his apology, and took back what he'd said.
Then, as he passed down the aisle
He added, in a stage whisper, to some of his cronies:
"If I'd said a half dollar,
I wouldn't never have took it back."

Betsy Endicott's Mourners

Jared Endicott and his wife Betsy
Lived in the square brick house
On the edge of the village.
It had been built by Jared's father;
And in it seven children had been born.
Now they had all moved away, or died, except Jared.
The demands of the large house had swamped Betsy
    Endicott,
And she had gradually dropped out of the village life,
Spending her days sweeping and dusting.
She kept the curtains drawn in the big parlors,
Lest the sun fade the red flowers
In the Brussels carpet.
Jared spent his days in his grist mill,
Where he sat at a high desk over his books,
Just as his father had done, before him.
He began to notice that no one came to call at the house,
And that Betsy seldom went out.
One night, after supper, he brought up the subject,
Concluding his remarks with:
"If you keep on this way, Betsy,
You won't have a Corporal's Guard to your funeral."

Not long afterwards he was amazed to see his wife
Stepping from the best carriage from Thayer's Livery,
In front of several houses along the street.
She would be received at the door,
Stay inside for about ten minutes,
And then proceed to the next house.

When Jared came home that night,
As he was washing at the kitchen sink,
He asked Betsy what it all meant.
With something in her eye
Between a tear and a twinkle,
She turned from the stove.
"Oh, I was just out getting mourners
For my funeral, Jared."

Abating a Nuisance

Judge Cowell was a just judge
And his decisions were based upon the law.
He was noted for his sternness:
A sternness sometimes overbearing
When a too full stomach overruled his head.
Court was sitting in Bennington
And the Judge had had a bad day—
So had the lawyers and the court attendants.
The Sheriff had been ordered by the Court
To stop the noise of unloading coal
Which smote His Honor's ears unpleasantly.
Then the clanging of the trolley gongs
On the Putnam House corner had aroused his ire.
Poor Wilson was sent to stop that racket.
The afternoon session was drawing to a close
When another sound was heard—
Just a gentle patter at first,
Growing, soon, into a disconcerting roar.
This was too much for the Judge.
He pounded his desk and shouted to the Sheriff:
"Officer, have that nuisance abated at once!"
Wilson arose in deliberate fashion.
"Your Honor. You'll have to apply
To a higher authority.
It's raining on the tin roof."

A Cure for Asthma

Taking everything into consideration,
Hen Billings was about the worst-looking man
The town afforded.
He looked like a hound dog in the rain;
His hair was long and straight;
His shaggy brows sloped;
His eyes sagged;
His drooping mustache hung below his chin—
A chin which sloped back into his collar.
He seemed built to shed water
Although he rarely got near enough to it to need to.
He had the "asthmy,"
And the poor fellow tried every new cure
He read of in his weekly paper.
Sometimes they gave him a little relief,
But more often not.
Then he would try another.

He came into Brayley's store
To buy a five-cent cigar.
Handing out one cigar, Brayley asked after his health.
"Fair t' middlin'," he wheezed.
He puffed hard on the cigar, and then carefully examined
    the ash.
"Tryin' a new cure for the asthmy."
Brayley replied from force of habit,
"What yu tryin' now?"
Hen blew out a cloud of smoke.
"WHISKEY."

The Clerk

Loren was clerking
In Hiram Woodward's general store.
Hiram not only sold everything,
He did odd jobs of carpentering,
And he had considerable repair work.
Loren helped at this, and clerked it, too.
He was handy with tools,
But too lazy to ache when he was in pain.
His efforts were largely mental—
Consisting of planning ways and means
Of avoiding payment of his just debts,
And methods of shunning work.

One morning a couch was brought in
To be repaired.
Loren was tending store
And after the effort of eating a hearty meal
From his dinner pail—he was a good feeder—
He stretched himself out on the couch.
He was reading the *Saturday Globe*
And smoking one of the boss's cigars
When Bingham, a young contractor, came hustling in.
"Well, Loren, you've got things pretty comfortably
   fixed."
Loren dropped his paper so he could see the intruder.
"Yes, by thunder,
And I don't no sooner git laid down
'Fore some damn fool comes in
And wants t' buy suthin!"

167

Bristles

Uncle Wheeler Millett
Was night watchman at Bradley's Mill
Down at the Borough.
Late each afternoon he'd start out
And walk the four miles,
And back again in the morning—
Unless he chanced to catch a ride.
He wasn't young, and the walk back,
After he'd been up all night,
Was a little hard.
He was trudging along one morning,
Swinging his empty dinner pail,
When George Bowers came past
With a pair of pretty good steppers.
George liked good horses,
And more than that,
He liked to show himself in a fine rig.
He never paid the least attention to Uncle Wheeler;
He just drove by in a cloud of dust.
When Uncle Wheeler reached the village
He dropped into Coy's shop as usual
To smoke a pipe and discuss the news with the cobbler.
He lit his pipe and watched cobbler Coy
As he waxed his thread and rolled a bristle onto the end.
"Coy, young Bowers'd make a good shoemaker."
He tipped his hat back on his head.
"All he'd have to do when he wanted a bristle
'Ud be t' reach 'round and pull one out of his own back."

168

The Road to Plymouth

(An incident in the boyhood of Calvin Coolidge)

Down the winding mountain road
Came a buckboard.
On the seat was a man, evidently a farmer;
By his side was a boy.
In a rack at the back
Was a wobbly, half-grown calf.
They went through stands of dark spruce
Where the chill of the coming winter dwelt;
Through woods warm with autumn colors.
The horse sat back in the breeching
Down the steep grade
Where the ledges rose high on either side.
They passed the three lakes shimmering in the clear
Sunlight
With brilliant spires of flame
Reflected along the shore.
Neither of them spoke
But there was deep intimacy in the silence.
As they drew near the town
The farmer clucked to the horse
And they picked up the faster pace of village life.
Nodding to all he met
He drove to the railroad station
And unloaded the wobbly calf.
He came back to the buckboard
Counting the money and putting it in his wallet.

"There, that calf is going to Boston.
If you work hard here at school
Maybe someday you'll go to Boston.
But the calf'll get there first."

In Jail

Jared Watkins was not a criminal.
He was too easygoing for that.
He would work just long enough to get a little money
And then he'd get full enough
To make himself a general nuisance.
A few days' entertainment at the expense of the town
Would invariably follow.
All he provided for his family
Was a little garden truck and a few cords of wood.
His wife took in washings
And when the children were old enough to leave at home
She worked out by the day.
Jared had been in jail for over a week
When he sent for the Selectmen.
They paid no attention to his message
So he stopped the Sheriff, Ed Collins,
When he brought in his dinner.
"Set down, Ed.
The town's got t' do some repairin' t' this place
Er it'll cost 'em money.
I've stood it 'bout long enough.
Now an' then I git spells o' walkin' in m' sleep,
An' I tell yu,
If I git to walkin', an' fall out o' this jail
An' break m' leg,
It'll cost this town suthin, by jiminetty, Ed Collins!"

A Little Careless with the Truth

We'd just made the barn with the last load
When the rain came down as only it can come
To relieve a parched earth,
After days too hot for living,
But just right for haying.
We unloaded into the north bay
And then sat and watched it rain
And let the fresh breeze
Blow through our sweat-soaked shirts.
Old man Peters loved to talk.
While he wasn't called a liar,
He was a little careless with the truth.
It had been said he'd rather lie
And give a discount,
Than tell the truth for cash.
Cutting off a piece of twist,
He got it limbered up between the words of his introduc-
    tion.
"Alfred," he began, "how long sence yer pa died?"
"Wal, that July, er mebbe a leetle later
We was doin' Hen Loveland's hayin'—
Doin' it on shares.
One day they come up an almighty storm
Jest like this one,
And we was settin' 'round the barn
Jest as we be now.
(That's what fetched it back t' mind.)

"We got talkin' 'bout liftin'
End I want t' tell you, when it comes t' liftin'
I was some punkins in them days.
Wal, 'twan't long fore it come t' provin'
What we'd been boastin'.
How they hollered when I allowed
I cud shuck thet load o' hay
By jest straightenin' up my back under the ex."
Old Peters dropped to the floor to show us
Just how he'd done it.
"I took in one almighty deep breath and lifted.
You wouldn't scurce believe it now
But I shucked thet hul durnation load
Two feet over against th' south bay.
Didn't strain none neither."

The rain drummed on the roof
And poured from the eaves.
One of the horses blew dust from his nose
With a loud snort.
Then Cy, who'd been lying on the bottom of the rack,
While old Peters was lying on top,
Stretched himself and hung his feet off the edge.
There was a queer twinkle in his eye.
He came from over the mountain
And his speech had a Down-East twang.
"Reminds me o' the time I was quarryin'.
A fella come from up No'th,
That made himself out t' be some strong.
One noon hour we was sittin' 'round
Neah a tahnation big block

We'd just broke off the ledge.
This young fella made a bet he cud lift that block
By pryin' with a baah.
Well, suh, he done some tall pryin'—
I nevah see a man try haddah.
Seemed as though his ahm swelled up
Double what it ottah be.
I ain't see a fella lift like that, nevah."

Cy slipped off the rack
And began to unhitch the nigh horse.
"Wal," said Peters when he'd got his breath,
"D' he lift it?"
Cy came around to unhitch the other tug.
"No, suh. He didn't lift it.
But say, Petahs,
His feet sank two inches
Right into the solid ledge he was standin' on."

Peters chewed a minute in deep thought.
"Look a' here, Cy,
You might jest ez well 'a' told me I lied
Ez t' told that story."

Thumb Tax

Folks scold about paying taxes.
Sometimes they pay them and never scold—
That's when they pay and don't know it.
The School Fund which helps out in the Borough
Came about that way.
Ten thousand dollars earning six per cent
Helps out when taxpayers are getting fewer,
And expenses are going up.

That ten thousand Enos Howard left.
He'd started with a peddler's pack
That soon outgrew his broad back
And filled a store.
Rum was a simple commodity then,
And Enos bought it by the cask.
He sold it by the pint—
Measuring it with a copper cup
Which had no handle.
Enos was a normal man,
But the thumb on his right hand
Was grown twice its natural size.
This was the means by which
Every customer's assessment was marked out.
With every pint he measured—
And those were thirsty days—
He stuck that large thumb down inside the measure
And gave a thumb-size less than the paid-for pint.
Year by year the casks were drained,
And every buyer paid his tax.

Ripe in years, old Enos died,
And left his family comfortably fixed.
Besides, he left ten thousand dollars
For the Borough schools;
A fund which yearly helps to teach the young
To read and write—
Things which Enos never learned to do.
Among the Borough folks it's always known
As "Enos Howard's thumb money."

The Blower Sisters

After Ma Blowers died
Mary was taken by Ed Squires' family,
And Ellen went to live with Widow Elkins,
Up the road a piece.
They spent their Sunday afternoons at the Squires'.

The dishes were all done
And they sat by the big open fire
Rocking and dozing.
They fell to talking
Of a neighbor who had died that week;
And that led the talk around to heaven.
They often discussed the streets of gold,
And the pearly gates.
Ellen, who'd always wanted to play the melodion,
Fancied the idea of playing a harp.
Mary spoke with yearning
Of days with no dishes to wash,
No potatoes to peel,
And, Heaven of Heavens,
Monday mornings with no washings to do.
Worn with such lofty flights,
They fell silent, rocking in the twilight.
Then Ellen, who couldn't be serious for long,
Got up and put a log on the fire.
"Land sakes, Mary,
'S like as not we'll both go to hell."

The Judge

The Judge had blue eyes,
A trifle faded but well lighted from within.
The radiating lines about them
Were ruts worn by many smiles.
Around his mouth were the same lines
So that all he had to do to smile
Was to turn the light on in his eyes.
He used to sit in his office door
And let the world go by.
He loved the cold logic of the law.
Now he was bowing before a law
From which there was no appeal.
And yet, content, he smoked his churchwarden
And watched the days slip by.

A young man was studying in his office.
He was a conscientious fellow
Who took life pretty hard.
One day when the Judge was attending court,
The poor chap had an awful toothache;
A swallow of the Judge's whiskey—
There was a good supply in the cupboard—
Held against the tooth would ease the pain;
But the Judge was too far away to ask.
In his sensitive soul there raged a conflict.
The pain raged, too, and won.

The next day, trembling, he told the Judge.
"Perfectly right, William, perfectly right."

The Judge turned over some papers in his hand:
"But I'm afraid, William,
That tooth may bother you all your life."

Henry Gets Trusted

Henry always worked—
At any rate, he went through the motions
When you were looking.
He was handy at almost anything,
And that, with an ingenious line of talk
And ingenuous blue eyes,
Made it fairly easy for him to get odd jobs.
He traded at one store while his credit lasted
And then transferred his business to another.
When all credit failed him
He'd go back and pay up at the first one,
And so on around again.

He'd paid up at Bonesteel's store
The week before,
And was getting a new account started
With a good supply of food.
He stood watching the storekeeper,
Standing at his high desk,
As he entered each item in his day book.
As Henry dumped his last package
Into an old bran sack,
He said:
"Bonesteel, when I git trusted,
Somehow I feel jest ez though
I'd had so much gin t' me."

The Odor of Sanctity

For over a year
Isabella had regularly attended Sabbath School.
She had learned the Golden Texts
And dropped her penny each week in the basket.
The sessions were held in the "lower room."
There were pews whose backs could be turned over,
And in the small enclosure made by two pews
Isabella sat each Sunday morning,
Listening properly to the teacher.
The room was rather dark and chill
And there was a shut-up, musty smell.
She loved to listen to the Superintendent
Because sometimes he called her name
When she had not missed a Sunday for a month.
As she grew older a "difficult" class of boys
Demanded much of her attention.
Finally, one warm June morning
She shocked her parents
By flatly refusing to go to Sabbath School.
They begged and teased and then, in anger, threatened.
She still refused and wept,
Burying her head in her mother's skirt.
Getting calmer at last, between remnants of sobs,
She said: "I don't want to go in there
Out of the sunshine.
It smells so of God."

A Wanderer

He had run away in his youth
Just to get some excitement.
The small mountain village,
Which was two miles from his father's farm,
Offered little except the yearly visit of a circus
And occasional socials at the church.
Somehow, after his mother died,
He didn't seem to be of much use at home
And he lit out for the West.
He worked at anything which offered;
He was a barkeep in a frontier saloon,
A stage driver in Colorado,
And then he followed the cattle trails.
When cattle rustling began to pall,
He signed up with a Wild West Show
And for fifteen years he had busted broncos
Under the big top in summer,
And worked in shops in the winter.

Now he was nearing seventy
And he delighted to sit on the back porch
Of the old farmhouse he had left,
And talk of this and that,
With just a glimpse, now and then,
Of those wild young years.
"Nope," he'd say.
"I don't never say much 'bout all o' that.
'Tain't that I ever done much I'm ashamed of,
But folks wouldn't take a mite o' stock in it."

He sat with dreamy eyes,
Gazing at the long ridge of Green Mountains
Which rose gently from the small stream
Marking the eastern boundary of his farm.
"Nope. When I set here on a Sunday afternoon
And think over all I ben through,
And then jest let th' almighty peace o' them mountains
Kinder filter inside o' me,
I tell yu
I don't more'n half believe it m'self."

A Witness

The trial dragged through the hot afternoon.
The tired jurors struggled to keep awake,
And the perspiring lawyers frequently refreshed them-
    selves
From the clinking pitchers of ice water.
Outside, the horses, fastened to the row of hitching posts,
Stamped and switched their tails,
And dozed with drooping heads.
George Mears had been examined by the State
And was undergoing a cross-examination.
The defense lawyer, unable to shake his testimony,
Had become a little overbearing.
He stopped and wiped his brow;
With deliberation he poured himself a glass of ice water,
And drank it at a gulp.
Then he turned sharply to the witness,
As if to cow him, and said in a loud voice:
"You have stated, Mr. Mears,
That you did not dance that night,
And that you did not partake of the liquid refreshments.
Will you now inform the jurors
Just what you *were* doing at that dance?"
George leaned forward in his chair and stared at the
    lawyer.
He settled back with an injured air:
"Why, b'gol,
I was the music."

Church Union

The village was used to divisions.
Although most of it lay along a half mile of street
One end had always fought the other.
It had been years before they had a town hall
Because each end insisted it be located in their section.
For years they had maintained two schools
Until someone left money to endow an academy
Located somewhere near the dividing line.
The Methodists had headquarters in the north end
And the Congregationalists held sway in the south.
In the matter of religion the division
Was not altogether geographic.
Finally, after years of fighting,
The town hall had been built in the center of the town,
And the academy had settled the school row.
The two churches continued in active competition.
Then, through death and removals, the Methodists
Found it difficult to keep things going.
They had to be helped from the church organization.
The Congregationalists were not too flourishing
And gradually the idea grew that the two should join
    forces.
After many sessions a plan was agreed on.
One of the first things undertaken
Was a much-advertised UNION SUPPER.
It was to be held at the "Congo"
Because they had a better kitchen.
That night there was an unusual turnout,
And even the generous amount of food supplied

Was hardly more than enough to go around.
Uncle Tommy Stevens who attended neither church,
Except when supper was to be had at a nominal sum,
Had eaten all he could gather and was washing it down
With his fourth cup of coffee.
As he finished it and sucked in his mustache, he observed:
"Wal, they say, 'In union there is stren'th,'
But I can't see it's affected this coffee none."

A Bridge to End Bridges

For some years
There had been considerable rivalry
Between the Kelly family and the Billingses.
Each family had its followers
And neither group allowed any chance to pass
To get the better of the other.
While it had started as a family matter,
It gradually got into local politics.
It was a demand of the Kellys
For another bridge across Otter Creek
That stirred up a rumpus at one town meeting.
There was a bridge less than a mile
South of the Kelly farm
And another about the same distance north.
However, the Kellys wanted one so located
That they could go straight to Rutland from their own
    farm.
A motion to build such a bridge, made in town meeting,
Had excited debate from both factions.
Just before the vote Avery Billings got the floor.
"Mr. Moderator," he said, "we already have built cov-
    ered bridges
At Goodkin's Falls, Ripley's, Patch's, Dorr's, and Bill-
    ings'—
Five bridges within two miles."
He stopped a minute. Then he shouted:
"I move we bridge the whole damned creek
Lengthwise."
The Kellys' motion was voted down.